Inventive

Movement

Margaret E. Anderson
Principal Lecturer in Physical Education
Hamilton College of Education

W. & R. CHAMBERS
Edinburgh and London

ISBN: 0 550 78801 8

Printed in Great Britain by
T. & A. Constable Ltd
Printers to the University of Edinburgh

CONTENTS

Preface   4

Part I   INVENTIVE MOVEMENT

1 The inventive movement lesson   10
Themes   10
Tasks   11
Limbering or introductory activity   12
Movement training or floor work   12
Apparatus work   13
End of lesson   13

2 Creating learning situations   17
What the body can do   17
Where the body can move   18
How the body is being moved   23

Part II   DEVELOPMENT

1 Limbering or introductory activity   29
Tasks   29

2 The development of themes   30
Transference of weight   31
Bending and stretching   48
Twisting and turning   57
Symmetry and asymmetry   66
Balance   75
Flight   83
Partner work   92

Part III   ORGANISATION
Prior to the lesson   105
Handling apparatus   110

PREFACE

The Primary school curriculum has undergone many changes in recent years and Physical Education has not been left behind in this exciting period of rethinking. We have moved far from the time when Physical Training consisted solely of formal work designed to exercise the joints and strengthen the muscles. Now that we understand so much more of the child's physical, mental and emotional growth, it becomes possible to relate his physical activities to his stages of development. When this is done, Physical Education plays a truly educational rôle.

It is generally accepted that the Primary school child should have experience in inventive movement (gymnastics), creative movement, games skills and where facilities allow, swimming. All these aspects of the total Physical Education programme are important and no one of them should be neglected in favour of another.

It is sometimes assumed that because this new approach to Physical Education is less formal, teaching does not require preparation or structuring to the same degree. This is not so. Inventive movement must be thought out and planned to ensure progression. Once teachers have experience of working along these lines and develop a pattern of preparation it becomes easier, as does work in any subject area.

Part I of this book enlarges on the principles of inventive movement and discusses in broad outline its various aspects. In Part II themes appropriate to the Primary school are developed. Sample lessons are given for each theme. The use of these, in the first instance, will give the teacher confidence in the initial practical situation. It is hoped that teachers will avoid the temptation to use these without prior study of Part I. A careful reading of Part I is necessary if the teacher is to understand the objectives.

It would be helpful to the teacher if she were to read Part III, which deals with organisation and handling of apparatus, before embarking on actual teaching situations, as this could well prevent difficulties in the course of the lesson.

M. E. A.

PART I

Inventive movement

Inventive movement

Inventive movement is concerned with the management of the body in meeting progressively demanding challenges and problems. It is concerned with agility of mind in thinking round the problems and with agility of body in solving them. Opportunity is given to every Primary school pupil, whatever his physical endowment, to *explore, discover, select* and *consolidate* his own ways of meeting the challenge of the particular movement task set by the teacher. This approach to the learning process recognises the pupil's need to achieve satisfying results. However, very little will be achieved if the teacher herself does not appreciate that it is she who has to create the situations which will stimulate the children to think and thus become aware of the movement possibilities of their own bodies. It is the teacher who plays a most important part in the ultimate success of each pupil. She is capable of observing the individual response to her chosen tasks, of encouraging the child to compete against his own standard and of giving experienced guidance. The results of good teaching are seen in the children's confident, lively and inventive movements both on the floor and on apparatus.

Primary school children have abounding energy. Their enthusiasm for moving, climbing and scrambling can be harnessed to well-planned and purposeful inventive movement lessons.

It is the aim of this book to give help and guidance to the Primary school teacher so that her lessons will allow her pupils, whatever their age and their stage of development, to become skilful in the management of their own bodies, thus giving satisfaction and joy which lead to self-confidence and poise.

Many students in Colleges of Education and teachers in Primary schools find inventive movement lessons very difficult to plan and carry out satisfactorily. This not infrequently results in the pupils being denied the experience altogether. The problems facing the teacher appear to be:

  (i) How to construct a worthwhile lesson;
 (ii) How to select the right material;

9

(iii) How to ensure progression.

One must first ask oneself 'Why am I going to teach this lesson?' 'What is my aim?'

The response might be one of the following:

(a) 'to give the pupils a change from classroom work';
(b) 'to exercise the pupils' bodies';
(c) 'to give enjoyment';
(d) 'to enable my pupils, through practical challenges and problems, to discover the satisfaction of success in bodily movement'.

If the response is (a), (b) or (c), or all three, the teacher can quite easily take the children to the hall and achieve her aim, but the time spent would be lacking in educational value. It is only when (d)—'to enable the pupils, through practical challenges and problems, to discover the satisfaction of success in bodily movement'—is recognised to be the aim and thus the true purpose of inventive movement, that it is seen that (a), (b) and (c) are merely incidental. To achieve this major aim a framework or lesson plan is necessary, each part of the plan being essential to the success of the whole.

1 The inventive movement lesson

Themes

A theme is a subject about which one thinks. This thinking about particular aspects of human movement is the basis upon which inventive movement lessons are constructed. This thinking is not over and done with in one lesson but is expanded over a series of lessons where the theme is examined from all aspects of *what* the body can do, *where* it is being moved and *how* it is being moved. By studying and developing a theme over a series of lessons the teacher is creating a situation in which the child is able to exploit his movement potential to a high degree. The solutions he arrives at from the movement tasks described in Lesson 1 will be used to build up experience and knowledge, thus leading him to greater understanding in the ensuing investigation of the particular theme which is being 'thought about'. The child is building his movement vocabulary and the experience gained is cumulative, bringing him to a greater awareness of his movement potential.

Remembering that when children begin school they are already experienced in running, jumping and scrambling over obstacles, one might reasonably ask why it is necessary to have a theme over a series of lessons rather than offer the pupils a variety of unrelated activities. However, the definition answers the question. A theme is 'a subject about which one thinks'. The actions with which the children are quite familiar have been performed without any conscious thought of how they were achieved. There was no question of: 'Is this the best way?' or 'Could I do this any other way?' In other words, the children's experience was limited to certain functional actions.

In the learning situation created by the teacher, i.e. her selection of a theme and relevant tasks, the child is required to think about what he is doing, to focus his attention on the way he is moving and to consider how he can increase his skill.

This focus of attention on a particular theme rather than on a variety of unrelated activities is necessary as it is in mathematics, for example, when the focus is on symmetrical shape. Unless symmetrical shape has been identified as the aspect which is to be thought about, there will be no understanding of the properties of shapes which are symmetrical.

By identifying the theme and developing it over a series of lessons, these lessons are linked together. Sub- or mini-themes are required to ensure the development of the main theme. They will lead to a more detailed investigation which will enable a child to develop his understanding of the concept of movement identified by the main theme.

Themes relevant to inventive movement in the Primary school are given in detail later in this book.

Tasks

Here the teacher seeks to select the best way in which she can create learning situations pertaining to the exploration and consequent development of the main theme. This selection will depend upon her assessment of her pupils, their age and their stage of both intellectual and physical development. The tasks will be such that each child, whatever his physical endowment, will learn and will achieve the satisfaction of success through investigation and inventiveness both on the floor and on apparatus.

A typical lesson has three sections, each of which will now be discussed in outline so that an overall view is acquired before the detailed planning of an actual lesson is undertaken:

1. Limbering or introductory activity;
2. Movement training or floor work;
3. Apparatus work.

Limbering or introductory activity

This is an essential part of the inventive movement lesson serving a threefold purpose.

(i) The 'large muscles' have been inactive in the classroom, therefore the body needs to be prepared for the activity to come.

(ii) There is a need to adjust from the confines of the classroom to the large space of the hall. This short period of limbering serves as a useful spatial transition.

(iii) Both the teacher and child will have to think in movement terms and to adjust themselves to using the appropriate vocabulary.

Movement training or floor work

As the heading suggests, this is the part of the lesson where the pupils work on the floor, experimenting with and developing the possibilities within the tasks presented by the teacher. By exploring the possibilities the child will discover his own solution and by so doing will increase his experience and his awareness of the variety of ways in which a challenge may be met. He then chooses one of these ways and by practice and repetition improves his performance, thus consolidating his experience.

Success, however, is not an instant and foregone conclusion. One cannot say that after the first few unsuccessful attempts the child has failed, but only that his success has been deferred. It is this deferred success which leads the child to think, to reassess the problem, to approach it in a different way, to try, to discard, to try again and so discover and be satisfied that he has reached his and therefore *the* solution to the task. In this way the child realises his own movement potential and uses this potential to become a skilful mover and to experience the satisfaction of success.

The teacher, meanwhile, must allow the child time to explore the possibilities within the task. During this time she is observing the movements of each child, assessing the potential and by coaching and guidance exploiting it to its utmost, so encouraging the children to greater experience which will increase their understanding of movement. Floor work is not an end in itself but is a 'training ground' for work with apparatus. The experience and understanding which the child develops on the floor will then be applied to advantage on the apparatus.

Apparatus work

Work with gymnastic apparatus is the climax of each lesson. As in movement training the teacher selects her tasks pertaining to the theme and, as on the floor, the child explores the possibilities within the tasks and comes to his own solution; the apparatus affords him new and more challenging ways of moving.

End of lesson

Just as the period of limbering is a necessary beginning to each lesson, there is a need for a short time to be spent at the end to prepare the children for the return to the classroom. During apparatus work the children will have been working in small groups, and these groups are made responsible for putting away the equipment. The time taken by each group varies, depending on the number of items used. As each group finishes, the children should return to work on the floor, thus making the class one unit again. The task selected should be one in which the whole body is involved and in which control and poise are emphasised.

Examples

'After replacing your apparatus, find a space for yourself. Practise balancing on different parts of your body. Can you overbalance carefully and roll over on to another part?'

'Start from standing and practise a series of curling and stretching movements which will lead you back to your feet.'

Lesson format

Teachers and students will find constructing a lesson less alarming if a simple format is used. This gives a pattern into

SYMBOLS USED THROUGHOUT TEXT TO ILLUSTRATE ITEMS OF APPARATUS

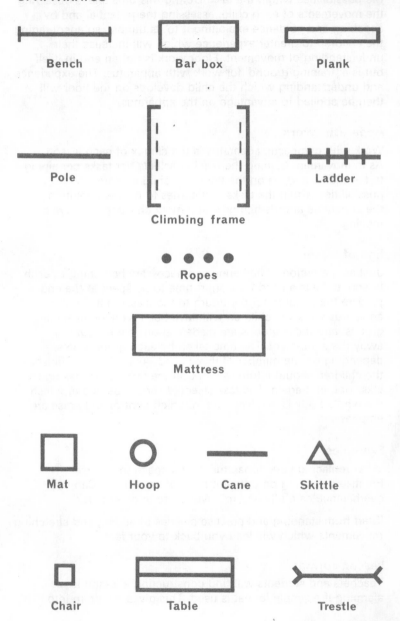

Bench

Bar box

Plank

Pole

Climbing frame

Ladder

Ropes

Mattress

Mat

Hoop

Cane

Skittle

Chair

Table

Trestle

which the material for the lesson fits easily. It also has the advantage of serving as a record of work which is easily read; and if a page is devoted to each lesson, one can very easily make reference to the material developed over a series of lessons on a particular theme, e.g.

Theme: Transference of weight   Week 1
Sub-theme: Pathways and directions
Limbering: Travel freely over the floor on the feet, varying the pathway and direction.

Movement training
Task 1: Curl up small and roll lightly over the floor. Can you change direction as you roll?
Task 2: Take a short straight run, jump high, meet the floor with two feet, curl up and roll over.

Apparatus work
Group 1   *Bench and two mats:* Using the feet only, jump high off the bench and roll over on the mat.
Group 2   *Box and mat:* Climb on to the box; jump off to land on the mat.
Group 3   *Two benches:* Travel from one end of the bench to the other, making a zigzag pathway.
Group 4   *Climbing frame:* Explore the frame, moving in and out of the spaces.
Group 5   *Mat, low box and bench:* Travel from one piece of apparatus to another.
Group 6   *Bench and two mats:* Practise rolling on the apparatus.
Finish: On the floor practise moving freely, sometimes curled up, sometimes stretched wide.

It is advisable to include in the format a plan showing the various apparatus arrangements. This enables the teacher to organise the placing of apparatus with the minimum of fuss and to use the available space efficiently.

A larger scale plan of the apparatus arrangements currently being used can be drawn and displayed in the classroom. The benefit of this is twofold as the children learn to 'read' a diagram or plan where symbols represent pieces of apparatus

15

and to recognise where one group's apparatus is to be placed in relation to that of other groups.

Older pupils who are learning to construct and use a linear scale could be given the opportunity to measure various pieces of equipment (length and breadth if appropriate) and, returning to the classroom, select a suitable scale and represent each piece by a simple line diagram drawn to scale. The next step

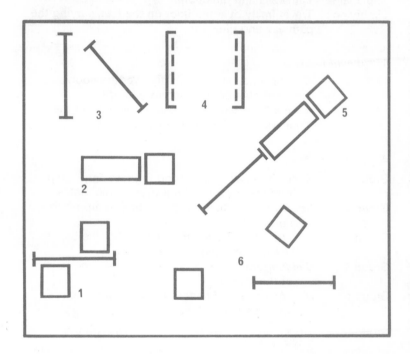

would be for each group of children using the same scale to represent one of the apparatus arrangements. Finally, the pupils will be able to draw the plan of the hall showing the apparatus arrangements on which they are currently working. This final stage may call for a change of scale to allow the hall to be represented to the same scale on the given sheet of paper, but this is a sound mathematical exercise as the pupils, being familiar with the practical set-up, will readily see the need for this change. It will probably be found in practice that, initially, the pupils select a fairly large scale, but this is all to the good as this is the stage at which they are learning what each symbol represents. When symbol recognition presents no problem they can handle a smaller scale and will enjoy doing so.

The symbols used throughout the text are those which children very quickly learn to identify. They are simple and represent, in the main, plan views of the items currently available in Primary schools. Teachers will realise that in certain cases the plan view is unhelpful in that it does not distinguish readily between one piece of equipment and another; in these cases certain modifications have been made. There is of course no reason why teachers should not use their own modifications where necessary, but it would obviously be helpful to the pupils if one set of symbols is used throughout the school.

2 Creating learning situations

The previous section dealt with the problem of the construction of a worthwhile lesson: the framework necessary for the lesson to have shape and form. The question now arises for the teacher: 'How do I select the right material if I am to create situations which will stimulate the children to think and so to learn?'

First there must be an awareness of movement itself. This awareness will enable the teacher to gain a real understanding of children's capabilities and needs.

The human body is constructed in such a way that it is capable of certain actions. Without making a detailed study of anatomical and physiological factors, it is possible to take a closer look at what the body can do, where it can move and how it is being moved.

What the body can do

Consider the first variety of possibilities which fall under the heading of *what*.

(a) Parts of the body can support the weight of the remainder, e.g. feet, knees, hips, back, shoulders, one knee, one elbow, one hand, etc.

(b) Parts of the body not supporting the weight can move into the surrounding space, e.g. when the weight is supported on the shoulders and back of head, the legs are free to move.

But in doing either (a) or (b):

Parts of the body can bend or stretch or twist, e.g. with the weight supported on the shoulders, the legs are free to move, the spine is twisted and the knees touch the floor beside the head.

17

Parts of the body can initiate movement, e.g. rocking action initiated by front of hips.

Parts of the body can come close together and can separate, e.g. as seen in step-like actions and in association with an external object.

Parts of the body can perform specialised functions—gripping, pushing, pulling, etc., e.g. feet pushing off from floor or apparatus, back of knees gripping bars on climbing frame, etc.

Where the body can move

The possibilities of *what* the body is doing lead us now to consider *where* the body is moving in the surrounding space. It is necessary to consider the two aspects of space with which the child will be concerned : personal space and general space.

Personal space

Personal space, as the name suggests, is the space belonging to the individual. It is the space surrounding the body which can be reached by all normal movements in all directions and levels without altering the base, e.g. curling up small or stretching as far away as possible.

General space

General space is shared with others. It is the working space : the hall, the gymnasium or the playground. It is the space into which the child moves when he begins to travel in any direction at any level. It affords great possibilities for exciting and inventive movements which lead children on differing pathways with changing directions and levels.

Use of general space

(a) *Pathways*

Children tend in the first instance to move round the perimeter of the hall, each child going on a circular pathway and facing forward. This tendency has an emotional, perhaps even an instinctive, basis : no one wants to cross a space which affords no protection. By placing the emphasis on pathways this tendency can very easily be eliminated. Young children gain great enjoyment from making recognisable patterns on the floor : these can be curved patterns, zigzag patterns or patterns which have been developed in work on shape in mathematics. The disadvantage in making floor patterns is that there is nothing left behind to look at! The teacher may give instructions about the pathway or the children may be left to make their own choice. They should, however, be able to repeat this pattern or pathway and to talk about its development.

Example

Teachers' choice: Travel over the floor on the feet, making patterns using straight pathways.

Children's choice: Travel freely over the floor on the feet. Can you make a pattern which we can recognise?

(b) Directions

Pathways which become floor patterns are but one aspect of the use of general space; another is that of *direction*. As the concept of pathways will encourage the child to make full use of the environment in finding out where his movement can take him, so an emphasis on direction will offer a challenge to his ever-increasing understanding of movement. By asking the question 'Can you go backwards as you move?' the teacher puts the child in the position of requiring to think 'Can I?'. A verbal 'Yes' is not sufficient, as children tend to give the answer they think the teacher wants to hear. The acceptance of the challenge of the question will be seen in the child's movement response. The concept of direction and change of direction should be introduced in simple form, as in the example above. The question could have been 'Can you go sideways?', etc. Where the front of the body remains facing the same way and the action or movement is already familiar to the child, the change of direction is an additional challenge and thus the thinking is directed towards this new aspect. The next stage would be a change of direction during a movement sequence, e.g. 'Curl up small and roll lightly over the floor. Can you change direction as you roll?'

It is important that in inventive movement these aspects of space should be stressed: they are necessary for the child to experience versatility of body management.

When using apparatus care must be taken in the planning of the apparatus arrangements and the selection of the task, if the emphasis is on change of direction. The dimensions of the apparatus should be taken into account, otherwise the children may be asked to attempt a change of direction on a surface which is too narrow, e.g. a bench attached to the climbing frame at a high level.

(c) Levels

In everyday activities—whether in the classroom, on the street, or in the house—the level at which one moves varies very little. This level could be termed 'medium'. In inventive movement the aim is to 'provide practical challenges and problems' and so to extend the normal experience. The challenge of moving at and through different levels is one which Primary school children enjoy: jumping high off the ground or rolling down a grassy bank are activities which can be witnessed wherever children play. The teacher can take advantage of such activities. Tasks can be selected which give children the opportunity of finding out how they can move very close to the floor, e.g. pulling and pushing themselves along, spinning and sliding. These activities close to the floor contrast with those of leaping and 'flying' through the air which make for movement at a high level.

Creating learning situations where the emphasis is on the exploration of both personal and general space will add much to the lesson. It is important for the children to learn not only how the space can best be used but also how the body can most efficiently adapt itself to movement within its space. The children will become aware of this space and of the possibilities for movement; and they will learn to work independently in the general space without interfering with the activities of others.

It should be noted that the aspects of space as outlined above make excellent sub- or mini-themes for young pupils, directions being emphasised in one lesson, levels in another, etc. As main themes to be developed over a series of lessons they lack the immediate interest and purpose essential for Primary school pupils.

Shape

Before leaving the 'where the body is moving' aspect of inventive movement, it is important to consider the shape the body makes during movement. Once the action is established the child should be made aware of the shape the body should make to achieve maximum economy and efficiency of movement. It is necessary to appreciate that the shape the body makes comes about because of the movement leading up to it. Shapes should not be assumed but should be moved through or into, and out of, during the sequence of movement. Unless the pupils understand this they tend to adopt statue-like poses which bear little or no relation to the movement which has gone before or, for that matter, the one which must follow.

Rounded shapes are those in which the movement leads into a curve towards the centre. This curve may be forward, and take the child into a rolling movement; or backward, when the body will become arched; or sideways when the body will curve or curl over one side to lead on to a tumbling action. The curving movement may remain 'open' or become smaller and more compact depending on what is to follow.

Long shapes are the opposite of rounded shapes. Here the accent is on stretching away from the centre, each half reaching out as far as possible and the body becoming long and narrow. Moving into and out of a long narrow shape is seen in jumping or in springing on to the hands with a momentarily long, 'cat-like' shape made in the air.

Wide shapes occur when the body is extended sideways from the centre and becomes broad and flat. This shape is seen as the child leaps from the box and shoots his legs and arms sideways to make a star shape. When working on the floor, cartwheel-type shapes are frequently the result of the child's efforts to be 'wide in the air'. Different shapes can be seen at different stages of a particular action, e.g. rolling backwards uses the curved or rounded shape initially, but as the legs pass the head they can be moved into a wide shape and the weight transferred to the

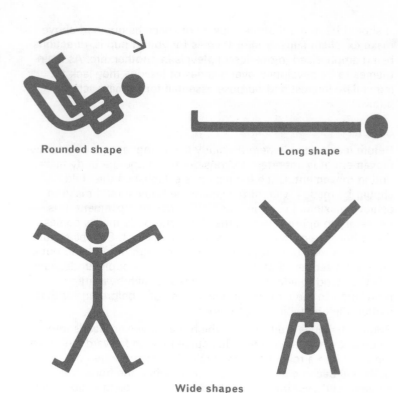

Rounded shape   Long shape

Wide shapes

feet which will be far apart. This frequently leads the child into an upright, long, narrow shape as the movement comes to an end.

Twisting shapes are made when one part of the body faces one way and the other part moves to face in another direction. This twisted shape occurs in rolling backwards when the knees touch the floor at the side of the head prior to the transference of weight on to them; or when an arch is made by taking the weight on the knees and one hand while the other hand leads the head and shoulders 'under the bridge' and the shape of the body becomes a twisted one. This shape is transitory for as the journey 'under the bridge' progresses to its climax the body untwists and most probably a long narrow shape will occur at the end of the movement.

At first it is not necessary for the teacher to place much emphasis on the shape the body is making as it moves, but as the children progress, she should point gradually to the relationship between the movement and the shape attained. Children will come to recognise the body shapes and to realise that the way to 'improve' a shape is to modify the movement which preceded the production of the shape, *not* to try to alter the shape once it is attained. The exception to this would be the deliberate changing of the shape of the body over the point of balance as a means of making balance more difficult or, conversely, the changing of shape to alter the centre of gravity and to make the balanced position easier to maintain.

How the body is being moved

Running, jumping, leaping and other such actions are enjoyed by most children. These actions take only a small amount of time, therefore the speed with which they are performed is quick. When a greater amount of time is taken, slow movements result. If the teaching of inventive movement is to be thorough, the pupils must have experience not only in the quick but also in the slow and controlled movements. The intermediate rates at which the body can move will also be used.

The teacher will **find when** observing her class that there is a

Twisting shape
(a)

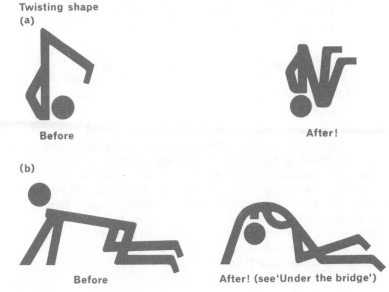

Before   After!

(b)

Before   After! (see 'Under the bridge')

23

great variety in the speed at which the pupils move. The task may have been 'curl up small and roll quickly over the floor'. Each child may be taking the smallest amount of time he can and so, to each child, the speed is quick. In other words, what is a quick speed for one child may be relatively slow for another, as each child's speed in this sense is related to his estimated potential. It is important for the teacher to realise this when coaching and giving guidance.

Tasks in which the emphasis is on taking a long time are difficult for very young Primary pupils. They have acquired neither the necessary understanding of speed nor the physical co-ordination and control. However, by the age of eight or nine they will have become sufficiently skilful and co-ordinated in their movements as well as more able to understand the concept of speed and changes of speed to be able to enjoy tasks that have this emphasis.

Resilience

Whereas the body is not resilient in the same sense as a rubber ball is, nevertheless its potential reactions are such that it is possible to land lightly and momentarily and immediately 'take off' as, for example, when meeting the floor vertically from a jump or in a series of movements involving a transference of weight from one part of the body to another.

For example, if the child rolls backwards each part of the spine touches the floor momentarily, the legs are carried up and over, and the feet or knees come in contact with the floor and immediately begin to receive the weight of the body to carry it to the upright position.

There is a smooth continuity of movement as each part which comes into contact with the floor 'takes off' immediately and there are therefore no sudden bumps against the floor. It is this gentle, bouncing-like reaction of the body that we call resilience. Teachers should consider the improvement of their pupils' resilience or 'elasticity' to be a main aim of each lesson. Ample experience should be given to develop this potential, because it is an important safety factor. The teacher should select tasks which will allow for the maximum amount of experience in 'taking off' from one part of the body to another. This is seen in tumbling actions, e.g.

24

(i) Running, jumping and rolling
 (ii) Running to dive and roll over on the mattress.

All movements involving a transference of weight involve the
body's resilience. By good teaching pupils will learn how to
tuck in the 'sharp bits', the head, etc., so that this safety measure
becomes habitual when they roll. They will learn how to 'give'
in the joints so that there is no jarring, and they will develop
the ability to 'take off' or 'bounce' from one part of the body to
another.

Once the child understands how to use his body's resilience and
to couple this with an ability to accelerate or decelerate and
change direction during a series of movements, he will become
aware of the inherent rhythm resulting from an interplay of speed
and muscular control. Older children enjoy the sense of
achievement which results from being able to control the body
in this way.

PART II

Development

1 Limbering or introductory activity

Movement tasks set for this three- to four-minute period can either have a direct bearing on the main theme or can be practice of movements already experienced. The task set or the choice offered should answer the requirements of preparing the child's mind and body for the activity to come. The instructions given should be concise.

The aim should be to get the children moving in a purposeful way as quickly as possible. The teacher should make use of this brief period to establish her leadership of the group. Moving freely among the class, observing the children's activities, offering encouragement and guidance she can ensure that all is purposeful and not just free play.

It is not sufficient for each lesson to begin with the statement 'everyone, practise anything you like'. The reaction is likely to be one which may become difficult to control as the children flit from one thing to another achieving very little. Thought must be given to the tasks for this period of limbering so that maximum use is made of the time.

The teacher will very easily become aware of the particular needs of her class. She will know whether certain pupils require practice in a particular activity, e.g. meeting the floor from a jump may be lacking in resilience; whether all the pupils require to concentrate on some aspect, e.g. making the best use of the general space; or whether she wishes the pupils to select what they feel is their own weak point and to concentrate on improvement.

The following tasks fulfil the requirements of limbering and will be helpful for the teacher at the beginning of her teaching of inventive movement.

Tasks

1. Travel freely over the floor, varying your pathway and direction.
2. Practise any kind of jump. See how high you can go.
3. Can you jump high and meet the floor facing another direction?

4. Practise taking a short run followed by a jump. Land on two feet.
5. Travel freely over the floor on hands and feet.
6. Work with a partner. One of you make an obstacle to be negotiated without contact.
7. Note where you are standing. Travel as far away as possible by moving from one part of your body to another. Measure the distance by counting the number of steps you take to walk back.
8. Choose a point on one of the walls of the hall. How many jumps do you need to get there? Try again and find out if you can cover the distance with fewer jumps.
9. Invent a sequence which at some point involves getting the feet far away from the floor.
10. Practise a sequence which involves rolling and twisting.

This period of limbering is of short duration, therefore the pupils should be encouraged to start immediately they enter the hall. The task selected by the teacher should be made known to the pupils before they leave the classroom or changing room. If pupils know what they are to do, they will begin purposefully.

2 The development of themes

The theme 'transference of weight' is basic to all inventive movement for Primary school pupils. It should be the theme which is investigated and developed first. If inventive movement is being introduced to the pupils irrespective of their age and stage, it is here that one should start. If a class is introduced to one of the more advanced themes, e.g. symmetry and asymmetry, the children will make very little of it if they have not experienced and investigated the possibilities of transference of weight. Such a situation would be akin to attempting to teach division before the child had learned how to subtract.

From work with Primary school pupils, College students and practising teachers on in-service courses, the following progression has been found to be the most satisfactory:

1. Transference of weight
2. Bending (or curling) and stretching
3. Twisting and turning
4. Symmetry and asymmetry
5. Balance
6. Flight.

This list may seem rather short for the total years of Primary school, but if the teacher looks more closely at each theme, the developments within each should become apparent.

Before looking at each theme in greater detail, the teacher should again consider the three words *what*, *where* and *how*. (See page 10.) Each of the following aspects leads out from the theme and is developed in detail:

   (i) what the body can do;
  (ii) where the body is being moved;
 (iii) how the body is being moved.

To examine each theme more closely, it is necessary to refer to the diagram on page 34 so that the total development may be seen.

This diagram serves, in the first instance, as a guide to the material for teaching; and as a check-up on the aspects of the theme already covered (so that those not yet dealt with can be very easily identified). This checking-up is necessary between lessons so that the next lesson can contain something new, since each lesson should offer at least one new adventure for the pupils. This 'new adventure' is achieved by the use of sub-themes which must change: firstly, if the theme is to be developed fully and secondly, as a new interest for the pupils to investigate. The main theme, however, can continue for as long as the teacher thinks is necessary for its development. This can be for half a term if the theme—like the basic one of transference of weight—is such that there are many avenues for investigation.

Themes are appropriate to work on the floor and on apparatus. It is essential that the pupils should understand this point. The teacher must therefore word the tasks for apparatus work in such a way that they are seen by the pupils to be a progression from the movement training they have developed on the floor.

Transference of weight

Transference of weight consists of two aspects:

(a) When the base which is supporting the weight is altered. For example, in walking, the weight is transferred from one foot to the other in succession. In rocking sideways on the hips, the weight is moved from one hip to the other. When balancing on the shoulders, the weight can be transferred on to the knees by the movement of the legs through the space; when rolling, the weight is transferred from one rounded surface to another.

There are many ways in which children can transfer their weight by moving from one supporting base to another and maintain contact with the floor or apparatus.

Loss of contact with the supporting surface—the floor or apparatus—when the base is altered, is seen in actions involving transference of weight. This loss of contact may be of very short duration as in springing from the feet on to the hands. Other examples of this change of base are:

1. taking the weight on to the hands, as in a handstand, when the feet were the original base;
2. transferring the weight from one hand to the other followed by one foot to the other in quick succession, as in cartwheel-type movement;
3. springing from the hands on to the feet is also a transference of weight with a change of base and momentary loss of contact with the supporting object.

(*b*) When the base supporting the weight remains the same.

For example, in a vertical jump from two feet the weight of the body is transferred upwards in the course of the action and the base is momentarily lost. The body then returns to the floor by the action of the force of gravity and the feet are once again the supporting base. Similarly in a crouched position the base does not alter but the weight of the body is brought nearer the floor, i.e. the centre of gravity has been lowered therefore the weight has been transferred. Hopping from one foot and landing on the same foot is another way of transferring the weight where the base remains the same. This same method of transferring weight is seen in the bouncing actions which children enjoy.

Sliding is not in itself a method of transferring weight, because the body is not actually doing anything except maintaining a position. Sliding is the result of some action which has gone before, e.g. a run, when the slide is a maintaining of balance on the feet. This is frequently seen as an enjoyable pastime during frosty weather. As proper footwear prohibits sliding on the feet in the hall, other surfaces of the body afford children similar experience, e.g. a run followed by a dive; a push off from the hands and feet and the child will slide along on his seat.

PARTS OF THE BODY CAN SUPPORT THE WEIGHT OF THE REMAINDER

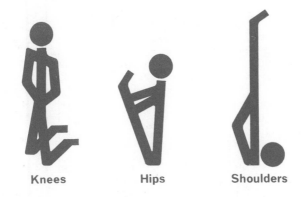

Knees   Hips   Shoulders

One elbow and one knee

Back

Hand and one foot

Rocking on front of hips

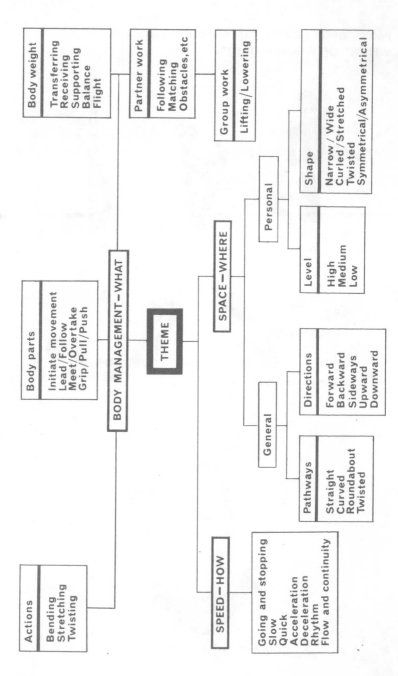

Actions

Bending
Stretching
Twisting

Body parts

Initiate movement
Lead / Follow
Meet / Overtake
Grip / Pull / Push

Body weight

Transferring
Receiving
Supporting
Balance
Flight

Partner work

Following
Matching
Obstacles, etc

Group work

Lifting / Lowering

BODY MANAGEMENT — WHAT

THEME

SPEED — HOW

Going and stopping
Slow
Quick
Acceleration
Deceleration
Rhythm
Flow and continuity

SPACE — WHERE

General

Pathways

Straight
Curved
Roundabout
Twisted

Directions

Forward
Backward
Sideways
Upward
Downward

Personal

Level

High
Medium
Low

Shape

Narrow / Wide
Curled / Stretched
Twisted
Symmetrical / Asymmetrical

Another means by which sliding can be experienced is seen when children are working in twos: one child pulls/slides the other between his legs; or one sits or lies on the floor while the other spins him round to let go at the height of the spin; this results in a spinning slide which comes to a halt as the momentum dies away.

We have already discussed the point that if themes are to be developed fully sub-themes should be used. If we take transference of weight as the main theme, the following table shows how this development can take place.

Theme:	Transference of weight	Lessons 1 and 2
Sub-theme:	Pathways and directions	
Theme:	Transference of weight	Lessons 3 and 4
Sub-theme:	Parts of the body which can support weight	
Theme:	Transference of weight	Lessons 5 and 6
Sub-theme:	Going and stopping	
Theme:	Transference of weight	Lesson 7
Sub-theme:	Parts of the body which can initiate movement	
Theme:	Transference of weight	Lesson 8
Sub-theme:	Quick and slow	

It will be seen that eight lessons have been allocated for the development of the main theme, each sub-theme being investigated for two lessons with the exception of Nos. 7 and 8. This is, however, merely an example of how a theme can be developed. Each teacher will decide for herself the length of time needed for her particular class. No one can state categorically that x number of lessons or weeks is the right length of time to be spent on a theme. Each teacher differs in her approach, each class is different from all others at the same chronological age, each child is an individual. This is why the material for each lesson is chosen by the teacher, as she is the one who best knows the needs of her class.

By consulting the diagram on page 36, the teacher will see that if transference of weight is the theme it is not difficult to select the sub-themes by following the lines out from the centre and identifying the appropriate sub-theme. Having made this selection, and ticked it off, it is then quite a simple matter to choose what will be next for investigation.

Thus, using the example given, the following aspects of movement will have been worked on over the eight lessons:

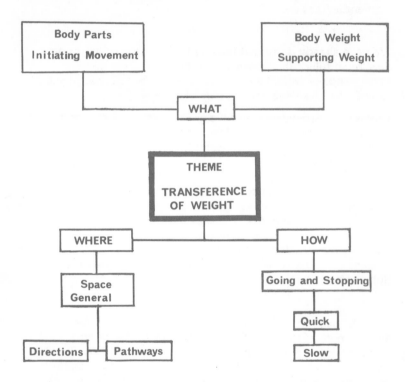

This method of recording ensures that no aspect which is applicable as a sub-theme can be overlooked; and thus the pupils are given a widely varied experience of movement developed from one theme.

If, however, the teacher wishes to develop a particular aspect of movement previously mentioned as a sub-theme, e.g. changes of direction, there is no reason why she should not make this the main focus over a series of lessons. In the diagram above, 'directions' appears as a sub-theme of the main theme (transference of weight); but changes of direction could become the main theme:

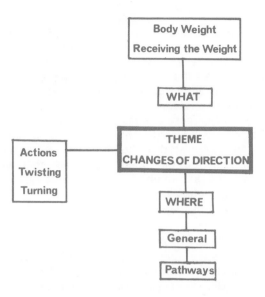

Theme:	Changes of direction	Lessons 1 and 2
Sub-theme:	Pathways	
Theme:	Changes of direction	Lessons 3 and 4
Sub-theme:	Receiving the weight	
Theme:	Changes of direction	Lessons 5 and 6
Sub-theme:	Twisting and turning	
		etc.

The essential for each teacher is to know why she is teaching what she is teaching. When a theme is selected, the development must be carefully chosen so that the pupil can progress towards an understanding of the concepts involved. This development must be planned throughout a series of lessons and if the format for lesson preparation is used and co-ordinated with the diagram on page 34 showing the avenues to be investigated, there should be no problems.

Children are individuals and must be taught as such; the teacher therefore must plan her lessons according to the potential of the individuals within the class. Tasks must be worded in such a way that there is opportunity for all to experience a degree of success.

There are many teachers in our Primary schools whose own training did not equip them for the great changes which have recently taken place in education. These teachers, though very experienced specialists in Primary education, find the planning of inventive movement lessons difficult because the material is so different from that which they themselves learned as students. It is for these teachers that the following examples of lessons have been written. The author believes that it is better for teachers to begin by using a lesson planned by someone else rather than not to begin at all. These lessons will be the foundation from which their own will emerge. They will see the pupils' lively response and, having studied the underlying principles of inventive movement as described in this book, they will be able to assess the present ability of their classes and to plan their material accordingly.

LESSON A

The first example of a lesson, the theme of which is transference of weight, is given on page 13 in Part I. The suggestions for work on apparatus indicate that there should be six groups working at six different apparatus arrangements. This great variety is not recommended to the young inexperienced teacher, since she is probably a little unsure of her ability to cope and is, quite naturally, concerned for the safety of her pupils in this situation. Following the section headed 'Apparatus work' on page 15, suggestions are given as to how the teacher can, by her selection of apparatus, become more quickly confident of her own ability and realise her own valuable role.

LESSON B

Theme
Transference of weight

Sub-theme
Parts of the body supporting the weight

Limbering
Practise any kind of jump. See how high you can go, etc.

Movement training

Task 1
Take your weight on to your hands and make your feet meet somewhere in the air.

38

Teaching: (i) The placing of the hands is important—about shoulder width apart; the palms should be *flat* and the elbows straight.

(ii) Stress the need for control as the feet come towards the floor, thus avoiding unnecessary jarring.

Task 2a

Find out which parts of your body you can balance on.

Teaching: (i) Time must be given to the pupils to experiment. Young children may require some hints to encourage them to take the weight on less usual parts, e.g. knees, one knee, one hand, front of hips, etc.

(ii) Encourage stillness of body over supporting part.

Task 2b

Can you travel over the floor taking your weight on different parts of your body as you go?

Teaching: (i) What is wanted is a smooth transition from one supporting base to the next. This will emphasise the 'take-off' as mentioned under resilience on page 24.

(ii) Decisiveness and clear definition of movement should be emphasised, each child being encouraged to move with an awareness of the parts of the body being used.

Apparatus work (See diagram of suggested arrangements on page 41.)

Group 1 Bench and two mats

Task

Move from the bench to the mat by transferring your weight. Roll on the mat.

Teaching: (i) Teach smooth take-off from one part of the body to another as pupils move from the bench to the mat.

(ii) Encourage children to share the apparatus, thus avoiding unnecessary queueing.

Group 2   Bar box and mat

Task

Use hands and feet to mount the box, move along the top, then jump off on to the mat.

Teaching : (i) Children should be encouraged to adjust the height of the box if necessary.

(ii) The pupils have the choice of how they move along the box. They should, however, be encouraged to experiment with different methods, having practised transference of weight during the movement training part of the lesson.

(iii) The jump off on to the mat will reveal whether there is 'give' in the hips and knees.

Group 3   Climbing frame with bench or ladder fixed across bay

Task

Climb on to the frame and travel across the bay using the ladder.

Teaching : The pupils should be taught to explore the variety of ways in which, by using the ladder or bench, the gap can be crossed, e.g. along the top, in and out of the spaces if a ladder is used, underneath by a 'monkey-crawl', or by swinging.

Group 4   Agility mattress or two mats, end to end

Task

Show as many ways as you can of getting from end to end of the mattress.

Teaching : (i) Children will probably roll from end to end of the mattress. Teach the 'curved back' for rolling forward or backward.

(ii) Encourage children to make use of both ends of the mattress as starting-points.

Group 5   Three classroom chairs (1, 2 and 3)

Task

Travel under 1, over 2 and under 3. (Chairs must be stable and suitable for use as items of improvised apparatus. Classroom tables also make good pieces of apparatus, but the same limitation applies.) The chairs need not be placed in the

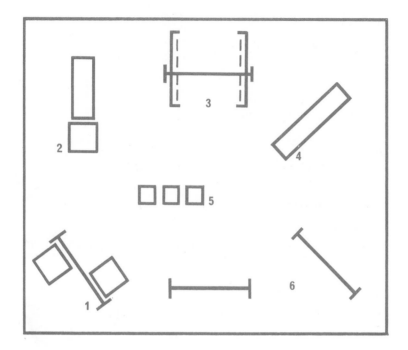

conventional position but laid, e.g. on one side, face down, etc.

Teaching : Coach the pupils to assess in relation to the task (*a*) the piece of apparatus to be negotiated and (*b*) the spaces formed by the way it is placed.

Group 6   Two benches

Task

Cross the bench with your feet as far away from it as possible.

Teaching : (i) If children jump over the bench, they should be encouraged to 'give' on meeting the floor.

(ii) If hands are used on the bench the main coaching is for the stretch of the body away from the bench, especially in the hip region.

LESSON C

Theme
Transference of weight

Sub-theme
Personal space—legs 'near and far'
General space—directions and levels

Limbering
Travel freely about the hall using hands and feet.

Movement training

Task 1a
Start curled up and as you roll sideways begin stretching to roll in a long narrow shape.

Task 1b
Run and jump high in the air. Land on two feet and roll sideways.

Teaching: (i) This is a fairly narrow task demanding an order of events but making the pupil aware of what his body is doing.

(ii) Allow pupils time to experiment but encourage a smooth 'take-off' from one part of the body to the next (resilience).

Task 2
Invent a short sequence showing a change of direction and a change in level for all or part of the body.

Teaching: (i) Time must be given for pupils to work out this task as it involves the selection and the joining together of appropriate movements.

(ii) Note carefully whether the movements are appropriate and the sequence is a flowing one.

Apparatus work

Group 1   Bench and two mats
Task

Jump high off the bench, land and roll over on the mat.

Group 2   Table top or chair
Task

Lie over the apparatus, place your hands on the floor and lower yourself down.

Teaching: (i) The palms of the hands must be flat and placed sufficiently far forward to allow room for the child to lower himself.

(ii) Encourage children to experiment with as many ways as possible of using their legs to help them.

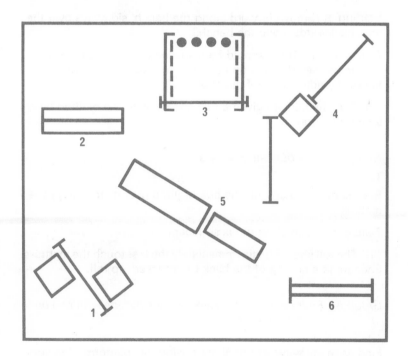

Group 3   Climbing frame, bench placed behind ropes

Task

Start from the bench, swing on the rope, then jump off.

Teaching : (i) The bench should be placed so that the children will have a reasonable distance in which to swing, but if it is too far back their hands will be gripping too low on the rope and their feet will touch the floor. Children should adjust this distance to their advantage.

(ii) Aim for a poised position on the rope and 'give' in hips and legs as the feet meet the floor from the jump.

(iii) The children should let go of the rope at the height of their swing.

Group 4   Two benches and one mat

Task

Starting at X move forward along the bench, sideways over the mat, backwards along the bench.

Teaching : (i) There should be a space between the items of apparatus (see diagram on page 43) to give room for the necessary adjustment of direction.

(ii) The children are given a free choice as to the method by which they travel.

Group 5   Low box and mattress

Task

Run, jump on to and off the box or jump over it; roll along the mattress.

Teaching : (i) A short run is sufficient.

(ii) The roll should begin immediately the feet touch the mattress. Encourage a curling of the back for a tucked-up roll.

Group 6   Four benches arranged two side by side with two on top as a platform

Task

Find as many ways as possible of using this platform. Can you change direction as you move along the top?

Teaching: (i) This arrangement is stable but children should be taught to place their hands flat rather than to attempt to grip the inside of the benches.

(ii) A variety of activities incorporating changes of level and direction can be explored, e.g. climbing on, jumping off, rolling along the broad surface, coming off hands first, etc.

LESSON D

Theme

Transference of weight

Sub-theme

Speed—quick and slow
Matching parts

Limbering

Practise moving about the floor changing from one supporting base to another. Travel sometimes quickly, sometimes slowly.

Teaching: (i) Smooth transition from one part to another.

(ii) It should be noted whether the movement is appropriate to the speed chosen.
(Refer to 'How the body is being moved', page 23.)

Movement training

Task 1

Take a short run, jump and turn in the air, land and roll slowly backwards.

Teaching: (i) The landing should be on two feet to enable a smooth transition into the roll.

(ii) As the roll is to be done slowly, the pupils should be encouraged to find out how this can be accomplished. (By a change in body shape, a more open curve with the legs stretching out to meet the floor is one way.)

Task 2

Try taking your weight on matching parts of the body. Can you move from one set of matching parts to another without stopping ?

Teaching: (i) Again one is trying to encourage a smooth take-off from one part of the body to another, and so improve children's resilience.

(ii) Children should be encouraged to vary the speed of their responses to the task, e.g. there may be a slow transference from knees to hips to shoulders to knees, or a quick transference from feet to hands to shoulders to feet.

Apparatus work

Group 1   Benches

Task

Cross the bench quickly, land and move away slowly.

Teaching: The teacher should observe whether the action chosen to cross the bench quickly is appropriate to the succeeding slower one. (At first children tend to use two isolated types of movement instead of assessing the task as a whole.)

Group 2   Bar box and benches

Task

Travel along the box, lower yourself to the bench and, keeping close to it, travel along to the end.

Teaching: (i) Pupils are given a free choice as to how they mount the box and travel to the end. The lowering of the weight to the bench will take much longer, since control is more difficult to achieve.

(ii) Some children may choose to roll along the bench. Others will pull themselves along or use some other method of travelling, but whatever the choice, the action must be carried out close to the bench.

Group 3   Climbing frame, ladder or bench fixed across bay,
bench inclined to floor

Task

Without stopping move smoothly from one piece of apparatus to another.

Teaching: (i) Children should be left to choose where they mount the arrangement.

(ii) By the nature of the arrangement, variation in speed of movement will result.

Group 4   Two benches placed side by side, two mats laid on top

Task

Approach the arrangement from any angle and use it to show any type of rolling.

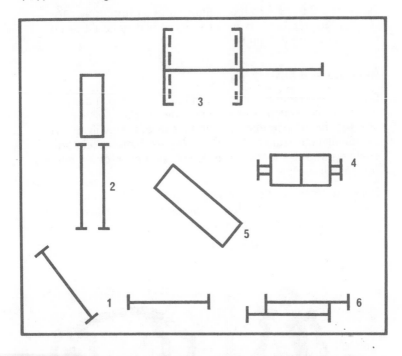

Teaching: (i) The mats will offer a cushioned surface for rolling either across or along the apparatus.

(ii) A table top would be most useful for this task (one mat would suffice).

Group 5   Mattress

Task

Travel from end to end of the mattress with alternately quick and slow movements.

Teaching: The speed should be appropriate to the chosen movements which must be in ordered sequence.

Group 6 Two benches

Task

Using hands and feet only, travel quickly along one bench and slowly along the other.

Teaching: (i) If the hands are on the top surface of the bench, the palms must be flat.

(ii) While the children are waiting for their turn, they can practise on the floor the various methods they could use of travelling along the bench.

Bending and stretching

Bending and stretching (or curling and stretching) are two of the basic movements of the body; the third is twisting. These movements are occurring all the time in everyday living. The anatomical structure of the body with its jointed skeleton enabling muscles to lever the bones upon each other, confers this mobility.

Bending of the whole body is brought about by a curling towards the 'centre', i.e. the spine bends and the extremities of the body are brought closer to the centre:

Stretching, on the other hand, is achieved by an extension away from the centre of all the parts of the body that are involved.

Bending therefore makes the body shape smaller and more compact; stretching lengthens or spreads it.

In the examples shown the parts of the body which are normally quite far away from the centre are moved closer together round the centre. However, both ends of the spine need not move simultaneously to achieve a bending or a stretching: the upper part of the spine, with the head and shoulders, can be moved down towards the centre while the lower end of the spine remains fixed; and similarly the lower end of the spine, with the legs, can be raised towards the upper half.

Lower end fixed

Upper end fixed
in jump with
bent knees

The structure of the spine allows for bending and stretching in every direction towards the centre, round about the centre and away from it to its farthest extent. Children should be encouraged to use this versatility to become just as skilful in bending sideways and arching backwards as they are in bending forward, thus increasing mobility and resilience.

Pupils should be encouraged to select different supporting bases from which their further investigation of bending and stretching can be carried out. The children will quickly realise that complete stretching can only take place when they are lying on the floor or on apparatus or when they are standing with their weight on their feet and their hands in the air; whereas curling can occur over a variety of bases, e.g. the feet, most of the back, the front of the legs and on either side of the body.

If, for example, the base is the back of the head and the shoulders, the bending will be of the rest of the body towards this base; and in stretching, the emphasis will be on a reaching away from the base.

49

As bending and stretching are fundamental movements of the body, the pupils will have used these movements many times already. They will have curled and stretched during their investigations of ways of taking and transferring weight. These actions will have been repeated without conscious thought, because the children's attention has been directed elsewhere, towards other problems within the tasks. The time for concentrating on bending and stretching as the main theme will come when the pupils have reached that stage of development when they are able to understand the concept of bending and stretching: this is usually when they are about eight or nine years of age. They are then able to understand and experience the sensation of curling inward as well as stretching outward from the centre or from the supporting base and to appreciate the necessity for accurate timing if skill is to be increased.

LESSON A

Theme
Bending and stretching

Limbering
Make up a sequence which has a slow part and a quick part.

Teaching: (i) This is a revision of a task previously met. The teacher will be looking for the order and continuity required to make a successful sequence.

(ii) She will also be looking for ways of responding to the task not offered in the children's first attempts.

Movement training

Task 1

Run and leap, showing a stretched position in the air.

Teaching: (i) The stretch wanted is a complete one, pushing as far out from the centre as possible.

(ii) If the landing is on one foot the pupils should continue to move forward, gradually slowing down or preparing to leap again. They should be discouraged from stopping suddenly, because if the weight of the body travels forward over one foot on the ground an ankle injury may result.

Task 2

Move freely over the floor with the body curled up.

Teaching: (i) Emphasise the centre round which the body is bending.

(ii) Encourage the pupils to investigate the different ways in which they can curl up and travel.

Apparatus work   (See diagram of arrangements on page 52.)

Group 1   Skittles, hoops and canes

Task

Travel in and out, over and under: sometimes curled up, sometimes stretched out.

Teaching: (i) The floor space linking the apparatus should also be used so that there can be travel from one arrangement to another.

(ii) Encourage full extension away from the supporting base.

Group 2   Two mats

Task

Cross one mat curled up; cross the other stretched. Can you join these movements together?

Teaching: (i) The problem here is the joining up of the curl and the stretch. The pupils will have to think of the arrangement in such a way that their movement on the first mat will lead into their movement on the second mat.

(ii) Suggestions from the teacher as to the direction of travel and the type of movement, etc. may have to be given to guide children towards a first solution.

Group 3   Climbing frame and ropes

Task

Half group—Travel up and down by moving in and out of the spaces.

Half group—Travel up and down the ropes.

(Half groups will change over.)

Teaching: (i) Frame: This task will involve a bending of the body as it moves in and out of the spaces. If the hands are crossed over and facing different ways, the child can pull himself either up or down and at the same time move into an adjacent space.

(ii) Ropes: Children should be encouraged to grip with the feet as well as with the hands. They should be warned against sliding down the rope, as friction will overheat the hands.

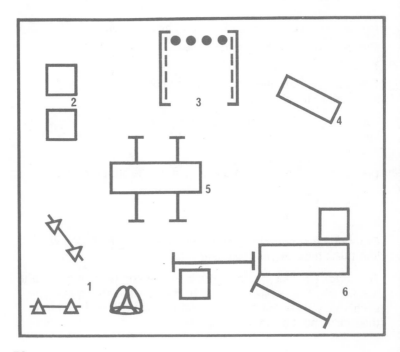

Group 4   Bar box

Task

Mount the box using hands and feet; get off by hands touching the floor first.

Teaching: (i) A strong push off from the floor will be necessary to arrive on the hands and feet.

(ii) The placing of the hands first on the floor will automatically bring about a stretching, but pupils must be encouraged to increase this extension as far as possible.

Group 5   Mattress laid over two benches

Task

By rolling, travel from end to end of the mattress.

Teaching: Pupils will probably curl up to negotiate 'bumps'. Encourage a variety of methods, e.g. elongated rolling; curl up close to the bench, and by stretching the legs negotiate the obstacle, etc.

Group 6   Two benches, box or strongly constructed table, two mats

Task

Use all the apparatus and explore the possibilities for curling and stretching.

Teaching: (i) Pupils should begin on any one of the pieces of apparatus but their actions must be appropriate to the structure of each item.

(ii) If jumping is used for coming off the box, a good stretch in the air will be needed followed by a 'giving' or bending in the hips and knees.

LESSON B

Theme

Curling and stretching

Sub-theme

Emphasis on parts of the body used to grip.

Limbering

Travel freely, trying to get the feet as far away from the floor as possible.

Teaching: Children may jump or, by taking their weight on their hands, attempt cartwheel-like actions. In either case the emphasis will be on pushing the feet away as far as possible from the floor, thus achieving a stretch.

Movement training

Task 1

Move into a curled position, hold still for a moment; move into a stretched position and hold this for a moment.

Teaching: (i) The holding of the position is important if the pupils are to experience the control needed, but it must be only a momentary hold, otherwise it becomes too static and lacking in vitality.

(ii) The moment of change requires exact timing. The children will become aware of this if the holding is buoyant.

Task 2

Select a space near one of the walls. Find out how, in this small space and using the wall, you can stretch and curl.

Teaching: There will probably be as many answers to this task as there are pupils in the class. The teacher should watch for maximum use of the limited space and full extension from the supporting base in the stretching movements. One solution might be a tightly curled roll towards the wall followed by a 'walking' upwards of the feet; another could be an inverted position on the hands followed by a slow bending at the knees and hips.

Apparatus work

Group 1   Two mats

Task

Practise 'collapsing' and tumbling over on the mat.

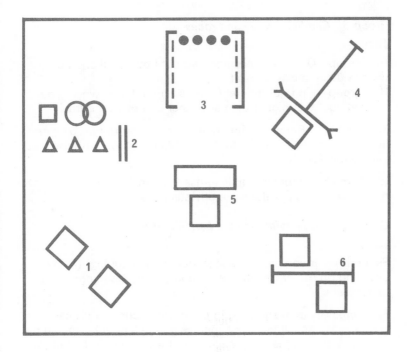

Teaching : Encourage pupils to release all tension. The body will then fall in a relaxed fashion on to the mat and, as weight is transferred from the part which touches the mat first, the body will roll over. (This particular task provides most useful training for safety; the pupils learn to roll over immediately they touch the floor.)

Group 2 Chair, two hoops, three skittles and two canes

Task

Arrange this apparatus as you wish and use your arrangement for curling and stretching.

Teaching : The arrangement set up by the pupils might require some alteration, but they should be allowed to find out for themselves whether the original is inappropriate for this task. By posing the right question the teacher can get the pupils to reassess their idea and then readjust the arrangement. It would be a mistake to alter the pupils' arrangement in an arbitrary fashion.

Group 3   Climbing frame and ropes

Task

Half group—Use two ropes and find out how small and how wide you can make yourself.
Half group—Find out different places on the frame where you can get your feet higher than any other part of your body.

Teaching: (i) Ropes: If the pupil is attempting to turn over and finding difficulty, a word about a stronger push off with the feet will be helpful.

(ii) Frame: Encourage pupils to use the corners and uprights of the frame, as well as the more obvious parts.

Group 4   Trestle with inclined bench and mat

Task

Find out what you can do, still stretching and curling, (*a*) by travelling on top of the apparatus, and (*b*) by travelling underneath.

Teaching: Children should grip the trestle securely with hands and feet. Many will use the bench as a slide, and they should be reminded to hold their feet away from the surface of the bench, otherwise they will jerk to a halt. Others will roll down when they feel confident of this method of travelling.

Group 5   Low box and mat

Task

Move from one side of the box to the other; roll on the mat.

Teaching: (i) Many pupils will be able to leap across the box; others may wish to climb on to it. Both answers are acceptable.

(ii) The pupils should be aiming for continuity of action.

Group 6   Bench and mat

Task

Find out how many ways you can use the bench to achieve height.

Teaching: (i) Encourage the clear definition of body shape in the air followed by resilient landing on the mat.

(ii) Question pupils as to how they achieved height.

Twisting and turning

Twisting is the third fundamental movement. Twisting occurs when one part of the body moves to face another direction, e.g. twisting the head to take a second look at someone who has just passed by. This action is usually referred to as 'turning the head' but because the shoulders and the rest of the body remain facing forward and only the head turns in another direction, the movement is, by definition, a twist. Another example of twisting would be seen when pupils respond to the following task: 'Take your weight on your hands, lift both feet off the floor and then replace them on a different spot.'

The hands remain fixed but in the movement necessary to place the feet back on the floor 'on a different spot' the rest of the body must twist, i.e. it moves to face in another direction.

Untwisting or unscrewing takes place if, in the above example, (a) the feet are lifted and replaced on the original spot, i.e. the twisted part 'returns' to face the same way as the base; (b) the hands are lifted and placed to face the same direction as the rest of the body, i.e. the base or supporting part has been moved.

The reader will recognise that in this case the untwisting has come about by a transference of weight on to another part of the body. Another example of untwisting by transference of weight would be seen in the response to this task: 'Take your weight on your shoulders and push your legs high into the air. Now by bending your legs try to put both knees on the floor on one side of your head and roll over to finish up kneeling.'

It will be seen that the 'screw' which occurs as the knees are drawn down beside the head is untwisted by a transference of weight from the shoulders to the knees.

Yet another way of unscrewing is by recoiling. Here the twisted part of the body 'returns' to face the same way as the base. This method of untwisting would be seen if a person standing upright were to keep his feet fixed and screw the remainder of his body round as far as possible then, without moving his feet, release the tension to allow a recoil and thus an untwisting.

In each of the examples given above there is a base which is in contact with the floor. Twisting can, however, take place when contact is lost, e.g. in a jump the legs can twist under the upper half of the body; or, similarly, the upper part of the body can screw round to face in a different direction from that of the legs and hips when the body is in flight.

When teaching twisting, it will be necessary to direct the pupils' attention to the fundamental concept that one part of the body remains facing one way while the rest of the body is 'screwed', otherwise they will fail to appreciate the principle involved, and an action which is not a true twist will result.

When selecting tasks involving twisting, teachers should note that there is little to be gained from asking the pupils to twist into a position, to stay there and then to untwist along the same path. This type of task would only be useful in the first instance to establish the feeling of being twisted. A twist should be used either to change direction and transfer weight or to twist or screw fully in one direction so that the recoil will send the body off in the other direction as in spinning. Once they have had direct instruction in the fundamentals of twisting, the pupils will be able to investigate the possibilities using as a base many different parts of the body.

Examples

'With both feet and one hand as your base find out where twisting will take you.'

'Try rocking on your front and find out if by using a quick twist you can move on to your back.'

'Move freely, stretching and twisting as you travel.'

Turning

In twisting, one part of the body is stabilised while the rest moves to face in another direction. In turning, however, the whole body moves round to face in a new direction or a succession of new directions. This turning concerns the whole body rotating round one of the three axes, i.e.

(*a*) The up and down, long axis (from head to feet). Turning round this axis will effect turning jumps, spinning on the feet or on the hips, and rolling with the body long and stretched.

(*b*) The side to side axis through the waist. Turning round this axis will result in rolling forward or backward.

(*c*) The front to back axis through the waist. Turning about this axis will give the cartwheel type of turning.

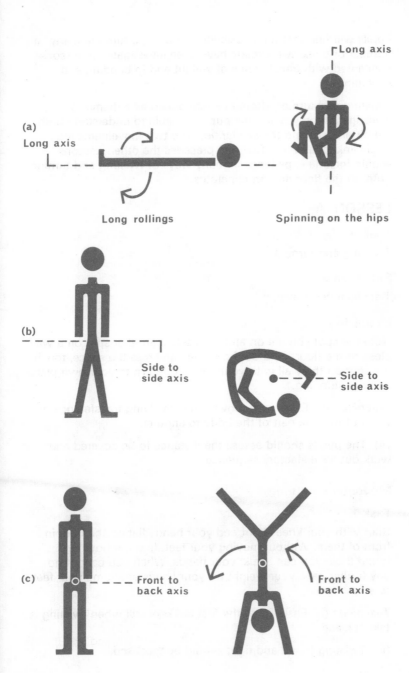

(a)
Long axis

Long axis

Long rollings

Spinning on the hips

(b)

Side to side axis

Side to side axis

(c)

Front to back axis

Front to back axis

Pupils will find that the possibilities of using a turn are many; a number of these will already have been investigated in lessons concerned with transference of weight and in bending and stretching.

Twisting and turning should be introduced as a theme for investigation only when the pupils are able to understand both the differences and the similarities. The two movements are easily linked, as very often one precedes the other. Lessons should include experience in many ways of twisting and turning both on the floor and on apparatus.

LESSON A

Theme
Twisting and turning

Sub-theme
Transference of weight

Limbering
Note the spot you are on and then select another spot on a wall close to the floor. Find out how you can cross the space, touch the spot on the wall with your feet and return to your own place without stopping.

Teaching: (i) Encourage movements involving transference of weight from one part of the body to another.

(ii) The pupils should assess the distance to be covered and work out a satisfactory sequence.

Movement training
Task 1
Start with your knees bent and your hands flat on the floor in front of them. Without moving your feet, find out how far round them you can 'walk' your hands. When you cannot go any further, take your weight on your hands and jump your feet to a new spot.

Teaching: (i) Ensure that the feet are kept still when twisting is taking place.

(ii) Twisting to left and right should be practised.

Task 2

Run, leap and twist in the air. Can you see your heels when you look over one shoulder?

Teaching: (i) By asking the question and looking for the response in the pupils' action, the teacher will ensure that twisting is occurring.

(ii) The jump and twist can first of all be done on the spot, making it easier for the teacher to observe the action, as the pupils will not be moving around.

Apparatus work

Group 1 Benches and mats

Task

Using all the apparatus, see how many ways you can twist and turn.

Teaching: (i) It is helpful in the beginning if the pieces of apparatus meet at an oblique angle, as the pupils will more readily see where a twisting action is appropriate. Also the task is simpler, as there is a smaller angle through which to twist.

(ii) This arrangement makes it easy for the teacher to give definite instructions should she find it necessary, e.g. 'Keep your hands firmly on the bench and twist on to the mat'.

Group 2 Box or table

Task

Find ways of getting on to and off the apparatus using a change of direction.

Teaching: (i) The pupils should approach the apparatus from all angles.

(ii) In the first instance they will probably jump down but should be encouraged to explore other possibilities of returning to the floor, e.g. lowering on to the hands followed by a twisting of the hips and legs to change direction.

Group 3 Climbing frame

Task

Experiment by gripping with different parts of the body (e.g.

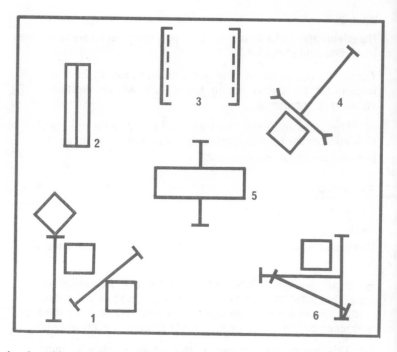

backs of knees, front of hips, feet, etc.) and twist in and out of the spaces.

Teaching: (i) It is essential that the chosen part of the body should be firmly positioned before the rest of the body moves into the twist.

(ii) The move into the twist should be slow.

Group 4   Trestle, inclined bench and mat

Task

Travel up the bench and come off on to the mat, showing twisting.

Teaching: (i) Encourage those who jump from the trestle to 'give' in the hips and knees on meeting the mat.

(ii) Some children may choose to climb down the trestle, showing twisting, when they will probably put their hands on the mat first. The hands must be kept flat and be placed well away from the apparatus.

Group 5   Mattress laid across bench

Task

Can you turn yourself over the 'bump' without touching it?

Teaching: (i) The pupils might 'dive' over the bump, in which case the take-off should be from two feet. Whenever the hands touch the mattress the weight should be transferred to the shoulders, the head being well tucked in and the back curved to facilitate the quick roll.

(ii) Some children may choose to turn like a cartwheel, when the emphasis should be on the stretch of the body away from the hands.

Group 6   Three benches and mat (T-shape with two benches, the third laid obliquely across the other two)

Task

Explore the arrangement by twisting and turning.

Teaching: (i) Encourage the pupils to use the space underneath the angled bench.

(ii) Point out where a twist would be more appropriate than a turn to achieve continuity.

LESSON B

Theme

Twisting and turning

Sub-theme

Weight bearing

Limbering

Select a part of your body you can balance on, twist on to another part and see if you can twist back to your first position.

Teaching: This limbering activity will enable the teacher to see whether the pupils understand the fundamental idea of twisting, namely the fixing of the base.

Movement training

Task 1

Practise travelling freely over the floor, sometimes twisting, sometimes turning.

Teaching : (i) Whatever actions the pupils choose to perform, they must be clearly defined. They should be taught to avoid a sequence of movement that could become ill-defined.

(ii) Encourage children to experiment with twisting which becomes spinning in the opposite direction; and turning (rolling) which slows down to become a balance from which a twist can transfer weight.

Task 2

Choose parts of your body which will make a bridge shape. Can you release one support and twist under the rest to take up a new position ?

Teaching : This task involves a considerable amount of muscular control to avoid a collapse at the last moment of twisting. This collapse can be prevented by a quick transference of weight.

Apparatus work

Group 1   Hoops tied together, skittles and canes, chairs and one bench

Task

Arrange your apparatus to suit the theme—twisting and turning.

Teaching : After observing how the pupils use the apparatus arrangement, the teacher may have to suggest other ways, so that a greater challenge is presented.

Group 2   Bench with one end placed on rolled mat

Task

Travel up the bench, moving quickly. Jump off to show a twisted shape in the air.

Teaching : (i) It is not necessary to stipulate that all children should run up the bench, but they should move as quickly as is possible by their method.

(ii) They should be encouraged to 'bounce' from the end of the bench to get higher in the air and so have time to show a twisted shape that is clearly defined.

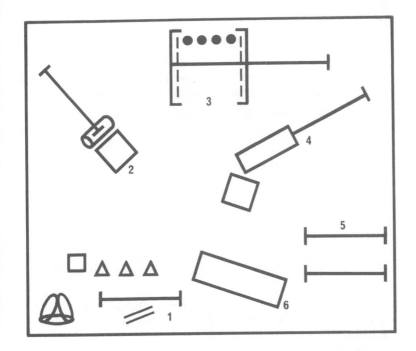

*Group 3 Climbing frame with bench or pole fixed across bay
and one inclined bench; ropes*

Task

Half group—climbing frame and attachments. Start by climbing
up the frame; travel along the bench or pole by twisting or turning
actions; slide down the bench.

Teaching: (i) Encourage the pupils to grip with various parts of
their bodies as they travel on apparatus.

(ii) Children will choose their own method of sliding but should
be reminded to lift their feet away from the surface of the bench.

Task

Half group—ropes. Practise turning your body forward and
backward between two ropes.

Teaching: (i) The ropes should be held about head height to
allow for pull and lift of the body prior to turning.

(ii) It will be easier to turn if the knees are bent up towards the
body immediately following a strong push from the feet.

Group 4   Bench, box and mat

Task

With hands leading, travel along the bench, twist to get on to the box, travel along the box and twist off on to the mat.

Teaching: (i) The hands should grip the box and be the fixed base for twisting. Initially the difference in height between bench and box should be limited.

(ii) Encourage a variety of ways of travelling along the bench and box.

Group 5   Benches placed with one end touching the wall

Task

Travel along the bench, take your weight on your hands and see if you can touch the wall with your feet. Twist off on to the floor.

Teaching: (i) The travel along the bench should cease a short distance from the end of the bench, to allow space for weight bearing on the hands.

(ii) The pupils should be encouraged to twist off to both right and left.

Group 6   Mattress

Task

Practise any kind of rolling on the mat.

Teaching: Aim at a high standard of performance in this task. In particular look for the change of direction; understanding of speeds relative to the type of rolling; and continuity of movement.

Symmetry and asymmetry

The shape of the body is bilaterally symmetrical, with each side of the body a mirror-image of the other. This symmetrical shape is easily seen when we stand with the weight of the body evenly distributed on both feet. When we are walking, however, the movement is not symmetrical, as first one side moves forward and then the other takes over to repeat the movement in exactly the same way. Walking is therefore an asymmetric action. Also, when we stand with one foot in front of the other, the shape of the body is asymmetric. Thus, although the body itself has a basically symmetric shape, many of the everyday actions it performs involve asymmetric movement, e.g. when the sides of the body are used alternately as in walking, running, crawling, cycling and canoeing or when there is an emphasis on one part or one side of the body as in writing, combing the hair, playing badminton or darts.

Symmetric movement is seen in breast-stroke swimming, or in taking off from two feet and jumping forward or backward, when both sides of the body do exactly the same action in the same direction and at the same time.

Symmetric movement can only occur in a forward/backward or upward/downward direction, because movement in any other direction involves an emphasis to one side and asymmetric movement results, e.g. if we stand with feet together and jump to the right, the movement is asymmetric, but at the end of the movement the body has regained its symmetrical shape.

To move symmetrically, i.e. to make both sides of the body do exactly the same action at exactly the same time, requires control and discipline. Children can become aware of the accuracy required to establish this relationship between one side of the body and the other.

Tasks involving symmetric movement should be introduced by using vocabulary which will help the child to understand the concept of symmetry.

(i) 'Travel freely over the floor on your hands and feet with your hands matching each other.'
In this task the symmetric movement is limited to the arms and hands. The teacher, however, must ensure that the arms and hands are being used simultaneously and are travelling the same distance with the fingers pointing in the same direction.

(ii) 'Travel freely over the floor with hands matching and feet matching.'
This task is a progression from (i). If the child keeps his feet touching it will be easier to achieve symmetric movement.

(iii) 'See how far you can jump forward, taking off from and landing on two feet.'
Again the pupils are restricted in the way they are required to move. This restriction ensures symmetric movement.

(iv) 'Can you roll backwards keeping the sides of your body level all the time?'

This restricted rolling will involve a considerable degree of self-discipline: previously, the pupils would roll over with complete freedom of action and usually a one-sided stress would result in the knees being brought down on one side of the head.

When planning lessons on this theme it would be a mistake to include nothing but symmetry in one lesson. If both symmetry and asymmetry are emphasised, the pupils will more readily appreciate the precision of the former and the greater freedom contained in asymmetrical movement.

When the emphasis is on asymmetry the teacher should guard against statue-like poses among the children. If, for example, a child takes the weight of his body on his shoulders and for asymmetric movement stretches one leg and bends the other, then after a moment in this position lowers his legs back to the floor, little more than an asymmetric shape has been achieved. As in the two previous themes of bending and stretching and twisting and turning, the value of working both symmetrically and asymmetrically is in the purposeful movement involved, not in the position achieved.

When the emphasis is on asymmetric movement the teacher should make sure that both the right and left sides of the body are being used, otherwise the tendency is for the pupils to use only their favourite side. This desire to use one particular side is seen when children perform cartwheel-like actions; seldom do they use the non-favourite side and when challenged to do so a marked lowering of standard is seen. It is important if versatility and skill are to be developed that both sides of the body receive equal emphasis.

Since all movement has to be either symmetrical or asymmetrical, it is necessary that the task states clearly what is required. A task which is worded 'Travel freely sometimes asymmetrically, sometimes symmetrically' is too vague and will result in a hotchpotch of movement. More appropriate wording for a task involving both aspects would be:

'Place your hands level with each other and try to lift the rest of your body high by pushing off from your right foot.' (This would be repeated by pushing off from the left foot.)

or

'Place your hands symmetrically and by pushing off asymmetrically from the floor lift yourself as high as you can.'

The persistent use of the words symmetrical and asymmetrical can have an adverse and irritating effect on the class as these words tend to sound pedantic and artificial. The teacher should vary her vocabulary to include such synonyms as even, equal, level, matching, odd, lop-sided, uneven, crooked, etc.

The terms should not, however, be ignored as the pupils must learn about these relationships of parts of the body just as they learn of symmetry in mathematics. It is useful if symmetry and asymmetry are investigated in the classroom at the same time as these relationships in inventive movement are being discovered.

LESSON A

Theme
Symmetry and asymmetry

Limbering

Keep your feet together and work on a variety of ways of travelling over the floor.

Teaching : The tendency may be for the pupils to jump with feet together; they should be encouraged to explore less usual ways of travelling.

Movement training

Task 1

(*a*) Travel forward or backward by placing the hands and feet symmetrically on the floor.

Teaching : (i) Discuss the meaning of symmetry as applied to the body.

(ii) As direction is specified, pupils will quickly understand that not only are the arms and legs working symmetrically but that the sides of the body match each other.

(*b*) Place your hands level and your feet together. Travel sideways on the floor by moving your hands and then your feet.

Teaching : 'Are you still moving symmetrically ?' By practical experience and discussion the asymmetric relationship of parts of the body will be understood.

Task 2

Run and jump, taking off from and landing on two feet.

Teaching: (i) An asymmetric run followed by a symmetric take-off requires considerable skill. The pupils should be encouraged to 'beat' the floor with the two feet on take-off and thus establish a rhythm in the run and the bounce-off.

(ii) As always when meeting the floor from a height there should be 'give' in the knees and ankles to avoid undue jarring.

Apparatus work

Group 1   Two benches

Task

Travel along the bench and come off on to the floor using the hands and feet symmetrically.

Teaching: Remind pupils that the palms of the hands should be placed flat on the bench. When coming off on to the floor, their hands will have to reach further forward so that there is room for the feet to land safely.

Group 2   Box and mat

Task

Start from X. Arrive on the box using the hands and feet, travel to the other end, and jump off showing a balanced shape in the air.

Teaching: (i) The box should be of medium height. Emphasise the take-off from two feet for the jump to the box.

(ii) Encourage pupils to jump up from the box and to show a clear shape in the air.

Group 3   Climbing frame and two inclined benches

Task

Move up the bench symmetrically. Travel through, up and down the frame by twisting in and out of the spaces.

Teaching: (i) Encourage a variety of ways of travelling up the bench.

(ii) Ensure a firm grip prior to twisting on the frame.

Group 4   Box or table and mat

Task

Arrive **on** the apparatus from any angle. Jump off **and** roll on the mat.

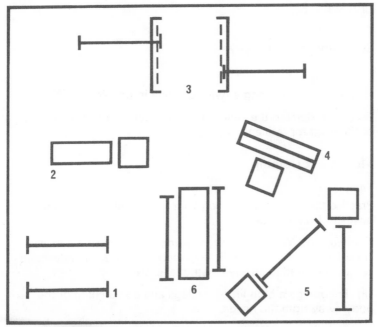

Teaching: Question pupils as to when symmetric or asymmetric actions were used.

Group 5   Benches and mats

Task

Roll symmetrically on the bench and asymmetrically on the mat.

Teaching: The pupils may choose to roll either forward or backward on the bench. These rollings will probably be done quite slowly to begin with. The children should not be hurried but should be given time to accustom themselves to rolling at a height above the floor.

Group 6   Mattress and two benches

Task

Use all the apparatus, showing symmetrical movements on one bench and asymmetrical movements on the other.

Teaching: After the initial period of exploration encourage the pupils to link their movements smoothly.

LESSON B

Theme

Symmetry and asymmetry

Limbering

Run and leap, showing a twisted shape in the air.

Teaching: Remind the children of the meaning of twisting and of the need for resilient landings.

Movement training

Task 1

Practise taking your weight on your hands with an asymmetric push-off from the feet.

Teaching: (i) When the task is worded in this way, no clues are offered. The teacher will see whether the pupils understand what is required in an asymmetric take-off.

(ii) Encourage a high lift of the legs and a stretching of the body away from the hands.

Task 2

Run and jump into the air, land on two feet and immediately roll backwards trying to keep the sides of the body level all the time.

Teaching: (i) The pupils should already have practised symmetric rolling prior to this task, which is quite difficult as there are changes in both direction and level to be coped with; and control is needed for the backward roll.

(ii) The push-off from the feet and hands must be equal on the two sides, otherwise the body will tip into an asymmetric roll.

Apparatus work

Group 1   Two benches and two mats

Task

Jump from the bench and show a lop-sided shape in the air. Cross the bench again by jumping from two feet to land on two feet.

Teaching: (i) Stress the necessity for height in the jump from the bench (unless height is achieved there is not time to hold a lop-sided shape, as gravity pulls the body downward very quickly).

(ii) Remind the pupils to make use of the swing of the arms to assist the jump over the bench.

Group 2   Low box

Task

Practise rolling symmetrically on top of the box.

Teaching: (i) Some pupils will mount the box and roll, while others may begin their roll by placing their head and shoulders on the box and pushing off from the feet. If the latter, emphasise the necessity for a strong push-off and lift of legs.

(ii) If overbalancing occurs, pupils should continue to overbalance but should stretch out the legs and feet to make contact with the floor safely.

Group 3   Climbing frame and pole or bench fixed across bay

Task

Find out how you can use the pole/bench (*a*) symmetrically, (*b*) asymmetrically.

Teaching: (i) Ensure a firm grip on the pole or bench.

(ii) The pole/bench can be crossed and recrossed, or used as a means of travelling from one side of the frame to the other.

Group 4   Trestle, inclined bench and mat

Task

Travel up the bench and jump off on to the mat, showing a symmetrical shape in the air.

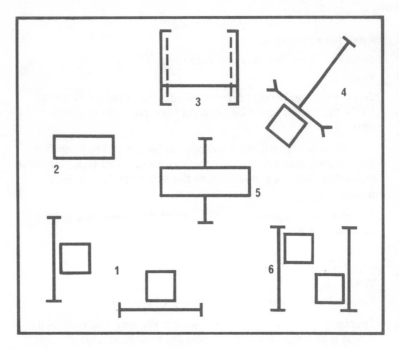

Teaching: Encourage the pupils to jump up from the bench, to show variation in the symmetrical shapes, and to land resiliently.

Group 5   Mattress over bench

Task

Cross the 'bump' with hands leading; roll to the end of the mattress.

Teaching: (i) The take-off must be from two feet. The hands reach forward to touch the mattress simultaneously when the weight of the body is immediately transferred on to the curved spine.

(ii) If, after crossing the bench, more than one roll is needed to reach the end of the mattress, it is the hands which must provide the necessary impetus to increase momentum.

Group 6   Two benches and two mats

Task

Show symmetric actions on the benches and asymmetric actions on the mats.

74

Teaching: The apparatus should be arranged in such a way that the pupils can move from one piece to another. Encourage flow of movement and clearly defined action.

Balance

Throughout this text the word 'balance' has been used many times. You may wonder why it now appears as a theme in its own right. The skill of balancing is in fact one of refined weight bearing. Previously the word has been used as a descriptive term rather than as denoting a particular skill. This is seen in the wording of the task:

'Find out on which parts of your body you can balance.'

This task is an elementary one where the emphasis is really on the parts of the body which can support the weight. Although the word balance has been used in response to this task the child may 'balance' on the shoulders and the back of the head or on the hips or on the knees and endeavour to bring the body to rest over the supporting base. The feeling would be that of pressing down towards the base, which is in contact with the floor. Having discovered the various parts of the body which can bear weight, the child must now find out how he can move from one supporting base to another.

In weight bearing the feeling is that of resting on the supporting base, whereas in balancing the emphasis shifts to one of lifting upward from the now reduced base. The size of the base is the deciding factor as to whether one maintains a relaxed stillness or a balance which is vital and dynamic. If the base is large, the weight of the body is spread out and the line of gravity falls easily within the base: therefore 'balancing' is not difficult. The smaller the base the more difficult it is to maintain equilibrium. When teaching children how to gain balance one must first teach them what 'to balance' really means. This can be done very easily by first asking them to adopt a stable position, e.g.

(i) Stand with your weight evenly distributed over your two feet.
(ii) Reduce the size of the base by taking your weight on one foot.
(iii) Reduce the base still further by taking your weight on part of the one foot.

(The position of the body will alter to keep the centre of gravity over this now very small base.)

In (iii) wobbling over the now small base will occur. Children who are beginning to learn what is meant by balance will need to experience the fine muscular control that is required to maintain a stable position and they will in the early stages either over- or under-estimate the amount of correction needed. Most children enjoy this feeling of competing against themselves and derive great satisfaction when they achieve their balance.

There are, however, some children who find balancing difficult. This may be due to a fear of being in an unusual position and one in which they feel insecure. Teaching balance work to such pupils requires patience, with guidance and encouragement being given, possibly over many weeks. The use of supporting surfaces such as the walls of the hall, the sides of apparatus or the teacher herself will help to give the necessary confidence in the early stages; but this use should not be overdone, as the child will begin to lean on the support and will not experience the feeling of balance.

Once the state of balance has been achieved, concentration is required to keep it. Often a position is 'moved through' so quickly that there has been no balance as such. Balance is achieved when the line of gravity falls within the base: the smaller the base the smaller the area of balance and the smaller the distance through which the centre of gravity may be moved without the line of gravity falling outside the base. When this happens balance is lost.

While balance is being maintained small, sensitive adjusting movements will be taking place all the time. As well as these small movements, larger ones resulting in a change of body shape can take place; these movements should not be made just for the sake of changing shape but should be the preparation for the next stage of coming out of the balance.

Balance will be lost when the line of gravity is moved outside the base. At first this loss of balance is often accidental, but as the pupils become more adept at controlling their body in balance, the shift of the centre of gravity is deliberate and loss of balance is induced. The pupils must then know which part of the body is going to receive the weight as it comes towards the floor, e.g. if the balance has been maintained on the right shoulder, the legs tilt over in the same direction, thus shifting the line of gravity outside the base. The right foot, followed by the left, reaches out to touch the floor and so take the weight of the body. There must be 'give' in the legs as the weight is transferred and the body adapts itself to the new position.

As balancing implies stillness, the pace of the lesson slows down as the pupils become more skilful. The tasks planned should be such that the pupils have the opportunity to gain and maintain balance within a sequence or phrase of movement, rather than continue with tasks concerned mainly with 'being balanced'.

LESSON A

Theme
Balance

Limbering
Travel freely over the floor, taking your weight on different parts of your body as you go.

Teaching: This task is one with which the pupils should be quite familiar. They should be reminded to transfer their weight smoothly.

Movement training

Task 1
(a) Stand with your weight evenly distributed. Can you make your base (the feet) smaller and smaller until you are balancing on a tiny part of one foot?

Teaching: Emphasise the lifting upward over the small base.

(b) Select another two matching parts of your body and by diminishing the base achieve a balance.

Teaching: Time must be allowed for children to work slowly and with concentration in their endeavour to achieve balance over their smallest base.

Task 2
Select one balanced position and find as many ways as you can of moving into it and out of it.

Teaching: The children should select a position achieved in task 1. To begin with, they may require help and guidance as to the timing of the move into the balanced position.

Apparatus work

Group 1   Mats
Task

Try to achieve an inverted balance at one side of the mat, then tip out of the balance to roll over the mat.

Teaching: (i) The pupils will need to work out possible ways of losing balance if they are to achieve a roll.

(ii) If there are one or two children who find this task difficult, a wall can be used to give initial support.

Group 2   One bench narrow side uppermost and one bench laid across at right angles, forming a see-saw
Task

Travel from one end of the top bench to the other.

Teaching: (i) The floor should be protected by mats placed where the ends of the 'see-saw' hit.

(ii) Encourage the pupils to control the descent of the bench by delicate balancing over the pivot.

Group 3   Climbing frame and inclined bench; ropes
Task

Half group—frame and bench. Travel on the frame and at one stage show your feet as the highest part of your body. Slide down the bench.

Teaching: Allow pupils to select their own way of getting the feet high. During the slide the body is balanced over the base. Encourage a variety of methods of sliding.

Half group—ropes. Try to balance between your arms. Can you lift your feet high ?

Teaching : The extra challenge of getting the feet high will lead to an inverted balance if taken to its climax. The child should invert his body with knees bent then, when balanced between

78

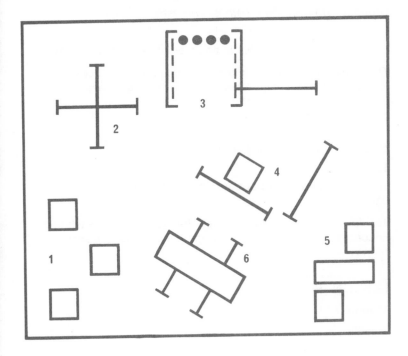

the arms, stretch his legs and change the body shape from curled to elongated.

Group 4   *Two benches (one narrow side uppermost) and one mat*

Task

(*a*) Travel along the narrow side of one bench.

Teaching: The pupils may choose to travel on hands and feet but they should be encouraged to try long steppings. If balance walking is selected, the body should be held in a 'light', poised position.

(*b*) Achieve a balance on the other bench and tip off to roll on the mat.

Teaching: This task is a contrast and so will have the effect of releasing tension. Teach the pupils to begin the roll immediately part of the body touches the floor.

Group 5   Box (medium height) and mats

Task

Slide over the box to finish in an inverted balance on the mats.

Teaching: The pupils must know which part of the body will touch the mats first and whether this is to be the base for the inverted balance; if not, there must be a 'giving' and transference of weight to the new base.

Group 6   Mattress over two benches

Task

Travel from end to end of the mattress showing at least one balance.

Teaching: Pupils should approach the mattress from each end. Encourage the children to blend the balance into the sequence of movement.

LESSON B

Theme

Balance

Limbering

Travel freely over the floor, transferring your weight from feet to hands and back to feet.

Teaching: (i) The hands should reach out to meet the floor and the arms must yield as weight is taken on them to avoid jarring.

(ii) If cartwheel-like actions are used, encourage resilience when weight is received.

Movement training

Task 1

Select parts of the upper half of your body to balance on. Transfer your weight and finish by balancing on parts of the lower half of your body.

Teaching: Time must be given for pupils to discover how they can move smoothly from one balanced position to the next.

Suggestions as to appropriate points of balance may have to be given.

Task 2

Invent a sequence which includes a twisting movement, a symmetric balance and a slow roll.

Teaching: (i) The order in which the pupils carry out the components of this task is incidental, but one movement must lead into the next.

(ii) The shape of the body during the roll should be such that a slow movement is natural to it.

Apparatus work

Group 1   Mats
Task

Choose a balance you enjoy achieving. Experiment with different ways of gaining and losing it.

Teaching: Encourage pupils to experiment, but ensure that they meet the mat resiliently as they come out of the balance.

Group 2   Box and mats
Task

Balance on the upper half of your body on the apparatus, tip off and land feet first on the mat.

Teaching: (i) The box should be fairly high so that there is room for the legs to swing down and for the feet to meet the floor safely.

(ii) Suggest parts of the body for balancing (hands, forearms, hands and head, shoulders, chest).

Group 3   Climbing frame and ropes
Task

Half group—climbing frame. Practise gripping with non-matching parts of the body.

Teaching: Ensure firm grip and encourage the pupils to stretch away from the frame.

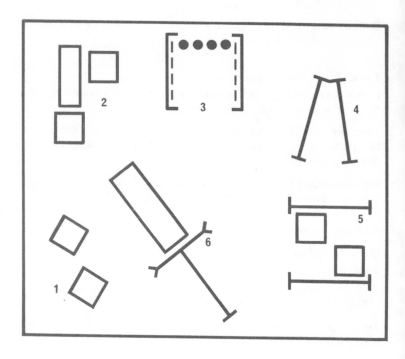

Half group—ropes. Swing on one rope, drop off and roll on the mat.

Teaching: The body should be poised on the rope. The drop should take place at the height of the swing. A relaxed landing prior to the roll on the mat is essential.

Group 4 Two benches
Task

Jump from one bench and try to land on the other.

Teaching: The benches should be angled to allow for differences in ability. As children become more skilful, the angle could be increased. Benches must be stable.

Group 5 Two benches and mats
Task

Experiment with inverted balances.

Teaching: (i) A secure grip under the sides of the bench will ensure a stable base.

(ii) Encourage the pupils to try out balances with one part of the body on the bench and another on the mat.

(iii) Remind pupils that they must know which part of the body will receive weight on the loss of balance.

Group 6 Inclined bench, trestle and mattress

Task

Use all the apparatus and show at least one asymmetric balance.

Teaching: (i) The balance is part of the sequence and should be moved into and out of without losing continuity.

(ii) Encourage the pupils to approach the apparatus from a variety of angles.

Flight

In inventive movement, flight is the term used to describe a particular kind of travelling in which one moves unsupported through the air. Flight occurs in jumping, leaping, diving on to the hands, springing from the feet to the hands and many other actions in which contact with the floor is lost. Children enjoy leaping and jumping probably because of the sense of freedom, the thrill and the excitement involved.

During this text mention has been made more than once of tasks involving flight, but now the aim is to examine this method of locomotion in greater detail.

The most obvious parts of the body to take off from and land on are the feet. The legs are strong and can most effectively propel the body into the air; the legs are resilient and can cope with the sudden reception of weight as the feet meet the floor. However, it is quite possible to 'jump' from parts of the body other than the feet; children enjoy bouncing from the hips, knees and shins.

There are five different ways (called the 'basic jumps') of using the feet and legs to propel the body into the air.

1. Push off from one foot and land on the same foot (hopping).
2. Push off from one foot and land on the other foot (leaping).

83

3. Push off from two feet and land on two feet (bouncing). This is the easiest method of taking off and landing, because two legs propel the body into the air and two feet provide a stable base for landing.

4. Push off from two feet and land on one foot. This is quite a difficult skill to master, as the strength of the double take-off and the resulting speed of the jump have to be contained on one foot in landing.

5. Push off from one foot and land on two. Here we have the opposite—a single take-off followed by a landing on a stable base.

Children should have experience of the five ways of taking off from the floor. These basic jumps should be mastered by the pupils fairly early in their inventive movement experience, the emphasis being on the method of leaving the floor and meeting it again and not on the time spent in the air. The main teaching point is that the weight of the body should be directly over the point of take-off, so that the strong push from the legs can lift the body into the air. The children should not, of course, be given the list of basic jumps, but should be made aware of the various possibilities over a period of time.

These basic jumps can be used separately or in any combination. Young children enjoy inventing sequences of two or more of the jumps.

The ability to jump and land safely is essential. Throughout their Primary school experience, children should be given many opportunities to develop resilience and control as well as the ability to jump in a variety of ways. This continuous practice is invaluable, as children who know they can cope safely when meeting the floor from a height will work confidently and competently.

The essentials of flight

There are three distinct phases in the actions which constitute flight: the take-off, the flight and the landing. Each plays an essential part in the success of the whole.

1. The take-off

The take-off or push-off is that part of the action which projects the body into the air, and can be likened to the releasing of a compressed spring. The hips, knees, and ankles bend; this is followed immediately by a thrusting against the floor or apparatus when the body shoots into the air. The change from the downward movement into the upward thrust is the most important moment of the take-off. There should be no pause at this point; if a pause is allowed the strong recoil of the muscles is lost and with it the spring. The depth of the downward pressure will be determined by the height of the jump, i.e. a small downward movement will result in a small jump, whereas a large jump will require the full use of the strong leg muscles: flexion of the knees and ankles will have to be increased, to give the necessary impetus.

This bending, which is the preparation for the upward thrust, is done fairly slowly; whereas the release-and-stretch action which projects the body into the air is quick and vigorous. The stronger and quicker this recoil the better.

2. Flight phase

This begins immediately the feet leave the floor. If the take-off has been efficient, the whole body will be extended and can remain so until the feet touch the floor again. The shape of the body can be altered during the flight phase; it can become wide when the arms and legs are extended; it can curl when the upper and lower halves of the body are brought closer together and it can adopt many symmetrical and asymmetrical shapes.

Flight can be vertically upward, or it can be directed forward and upward or sideways and upward. This decision must be made during the take-off phase, as once the body is in the air it can alter its shape but not its flight path.

The quality of flight can be seen in the poised, 'alive' shape of the body as it travels, if only briefly, through the air.

3. Landing

Much has already been said about landings and recoveries but as it is essential that children learn how to cope with themselves when they land, further consideration will not go amiss.

Although it is possible to land on other parts of the body, the feet are most commonly used and the principles involved are the same. The preparation for landing must start while the body is still in the air, e.g. the feet will begin to reach out towards the floor and immediately they touch the floor the feet, knees and ankles 'give' so that the shock of impact is absorbed. This bending of the knees and ankles is similar to the preparation for the initial take-off and thus it can be used as such to send the body up into another jump. If, however, a return to standing is desired the 'giving' or yielding of the feet, knees and ankles is followed by a resilient recovery without the strong thrust required in the previous case. There is a third possibility: if the 'giving' in the legs and feet is maximum, carrying the body close to the floor, the movement may be converted into a roll.

4. Flight from apparatus

It should be remembered that no matter how high the apparatus, flight will not be achieved if the children just drop down from the apparatus. The three phases of flight must apply—the take-off, the time in the air, the landing—whether the take-off is from the floor or from apparatus.

LESSON A

Theme

Flight

Limbering

(a) Travel over the floor by bouncing from two feet to two feet.

Teaching: Emphasise 'giving' at knees and ankles to achieve resilient, continuous bouncing. This activity is strenuous and should not be continued for too long.

(b) Practise springing from the feet to the hands.

Teaching: Emphasise the strong push-off from and the resilient landing on the feet.

Movement training

Task 1

Run and jump high, meet the floor with two feet and roll over.

Teaching: (i) A short run is all that is necessary when height is wanted. There must be a strong push-off from the feet with the upper half of the body taking part in this upward thrust.

(ii) Maximum 'give' in knees and ankles is required prior to the rolling action.

Task 2

Find out how many ways you can 'fly' your legs through the air.

Teaching: (i) There should be cartwheel-like actions, catsprings when the legs whip from behind to come close to the hands, and all forms of leaping. If the legs are to 'fly', they should give the impression of reaching away from the body.

Apparatus work

Group 1 Inclined bench, trestle and mat
Task

Move quickly up the bench and jump off on to the mat.

Teaching: Encourage a strong thrust of the whole body on the take-off. Ensure maximum 'give' in feet, ankles and knees on meeting the mat.

Group 2 Two mats, one rolled and placed under the end of one inclined bench
Task

Run up the bench, spring off and on landing roll on the mat.

Teaching: Take off from the bench on two feet; encourage a strong push down on the end of the bench to gain maximum upthrust.

Group 3 Climbing frame, ropes and mats
Task

Half group—climbing frame. Run and leap on to the frame; jump off at a height of your own choosing.

Teaching: (i) The jump on to the frame may be from either two feet or one foot. As the feet push off from the floor, the hands swing forward and upward to grip the frame.

(ii) If one or two of the pupils find this too difficult they should climb to a height of their choice and then jump off.
Half group—ropes. Swing on the rope and 'fly' off on to the mat.

Teaching: The jump-off is best done at the height of the swing. Encourage the pupils to move quickly into a roll, either forward or backward, if balance is lost on meeting the mat.

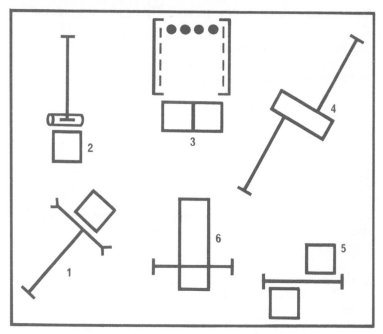

Group 4   Bar box and two inclined benches

Task

Travel up the bench and jump off the box, showing a clear-cut shape in the air.

Teaching: When the apparatus is arranged in this way, two children can use the box at any one time. Encourage a variety of ways of travelling up the bench and of shapes in the air.

Group 5   Bench and two mats

Task

Find ways of crossing the bench so that your legs 'fly' through the air.

Teaching: Encourage pupils to use the responses to task 2 of 'movement training' (p. 87), as the same points apply.

Group 6   Bench and mattress

Task

Cross the bench without touching it and travel quickly to the end of the mattress.

Teaching: This task allows pupils considerable choice. Look for resilience and continuity in the movements.

LESSON B

Theme

Flight

Limbering

Use your feet to 'fly' into the air. Follow the landing by an action which keeps you close to the floor.

Teaching: (i) The body should shoot into the air, the head and chest lifting as the feet thrust away from the floor.

(ii) There must be a smooth transition from the landing to the next action which will probably be some kind of rolling or transfer of weight on to the hands.

Movement training

Task 1

Find out if you can jump from parts of the body other than the feet.

Teaching: The pupils will discover that they can take off from the hands, hips, shins, etc. The body must press down over the base and then immediately thrust away from the floor. The weight will either be received again by the same part or be transferred to another, e.g. pushing off from the shins to land on the feet.

Task 2

Select a part of your body on which you can balance, overbalance into a roll and quickly come up to standing.

Teaching: Although flight does not come into this task, the pupils are practising smooth recovery from rolling to standing, which is a skill necessary for safety in landing.

Apparatus work

Group 1   Two benches and mats

Task

Use the bench to get the feet high.

Teaching: (i) The pupils may place their hands on the bench and 'fly' their legs through the air, in which case the emphasis is on a strong extension of the body away from the hands. They may push off from the bench with their feet: in this case look for a clearly defined shape in the air.

(ii) The landing must be resilient no matter what precedes it.

Group 2   Trestle, two inclined benches, and mats

Task

Use all the apparatus and finish your sequence by rolling on a mat.

Teaching: Encourage a variety of actions which will result in a flowing sequence.

Group 3   Climbing frame; ladder and pole or two benches
across bay at different levels; inclined bench and mats

Task

Use all the apparatus and finish by landing on a mat.

Teaching: The pupils have a wide choice in how they use this arrangement. It gives the opportunity for changing levels and directions. Ensure careful but continuous movement throughout.

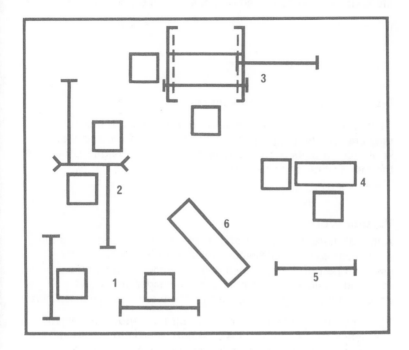

Group 4 Low box and mats
Task

Run and jump on to and off, or over, the box; land and roll on the mat.

Teaching: The length and breadth of the box should be used. In the former the jump will be on to the end; in the latter it will be across and over. In each case the arrival is on the feet only.

Group 5 Two benches, one superimposed on the other
Task

Find different ways of jumping over the apparatus, using the hands on the bench.

Teaching: (i) The hands should grip the edges of the bench if a crouch jump is used. If, however, the body faces upwards and the jump is of the scissor-type (one leg following the other) the hands should be placed flat, one after the other, on the bench.

(ii) Encourage a strong push away from the hands.

Group 6   Mattress

Task

Practise bouncing from different parts of the body.

Teaching: Allow children to 'play' with this task, but ensure that they are selecting appropriate bases to spring from and that they know which parts of the body will receive the weight. Otherwise the task will cease to be purposeful.

Partner work

Although partner work is not a theme in the same sense as the movement and action themes previously discussed, it is an essential part of the total inventive movement programme requiring an allocation of time and a consideration of its development. It is in this sense that the word theme is used here.

Partner work affords an opportunity for the various movement and action themes to be worked out in association with another person. Self-control, anticipation of another's actions, and co-operation are all of great importance. Partner work is therefore a theme which follows individual experience and is appropriate only to those who have already profited from this primary experience. It is concerned with the movement situations which result from working with another person rather than the development of a particular aspect of movement.

In situations where there is a shortage of apparatus, partner work can partially overcome this difficulty when a person becomes an obstacle to be negotiated or a support from which one can push off into flight, or in a situation where two people are better than one.

Working with a partner should be introduced only when the pupils are ready for this close-knit co-operation. Infants are very self-centred and are only interested in 'me and my movement'. This is a stage in their development and it would serve no useful purpose to put them into a partner situation. Working with another person involves a high degree of accuracy and timing and therefore the pupils must be skilled in these essentials as individuals before they can be expected to co-operate successfully with another person.

Children should normally choose their own partners, as friends enjoy working together and will create an atmosphere of give-and-take. If one child is less able and they have chosen to work together the more able child will help, will adjust his movements or actions to suit and generally encourage the other to achieve a greater degree of inventiveness and a higher standard of performance. If, however, the children are paired off in an arbitrary manner, the teacher cannot expect the same sense of helpful co-operation.

Partners can work together with or without touching. It is advisable for the pupils to begin working in twos without contact as they will take some time to become accustomed to this relationship: previously they had to be concerned with themselves as individuals within a group. While working as individuals they have learned to share the space and the apparatus but have been little influenced by any other child's actions.

Working with a partner without contact

1. Follow the leader

Most children are familiar with this type of relationship.
At first it is sufficient for *B* to follow *A*'s pathway exactly without being required to copy the actions accurately, e.g. in twos:
A moves over the floor making a zigzag pathway; *B* follows by travelling on the same track.

Once the idea has been mastered *B* attempts to copy the actions performed by *A*, e.g. *A* travels freely on the hands and feet; *B* follows on the same track in the same manner.

The pupils are working simultaneously with only a small gap between them.

2. Matching actions

This involves two children doing exactly the same action at exactly the same time.

(*a*) Side by side and facing in the same direction is the easiest way to match actions as the pair can see each other and keep level, e.g. in twos: start level and work on a movement sequence which involves a slow roll backwards.

(*b*) Side by side and facing in the opposite direction is much more difficult as there will be moments when the partners will be unable to see each other, e.g. in twos: select two matching parts you can balance on. Invent a sequence in which you start and finish in the same balanced position.

(*c*) Facing each other will give matching actions which are either mirror-image relationships, i.e. when one partner moves to the left the other moves to the right, or same-side movements, in which case the partners move away from each other, e.g.
(i) In twos. Face each other and keep level all the time. Use asymmetrical movements and invent a short sequence which starts from and finishes on the feet.
(ii) In twos facing each other. Make up a sequence of symmetrical actions which start and finish on the feet.

(*d*) One behind the other facing in the same direction as in 'follow the leader', but instead of working simultaneously the pair move in canon. Children enjoy the rhythm of this type of partner work, e.g.

Pupil *A*	Pupil *B*
1. Springs from feet to hands	————
2. and rolls forward	1. Springs from feet to hands
3. to finish on the feet.	2. and rolls forward
————	3. to finish on the feet.

If this pattern is repeated several times, a pleasing rhythm is established.

3. Partners as obstacles

One of the partners makes himself into an obstacle to be negotiated by the other.

Examples

  (i) *A* makes a curled shape which his partner negotiates without contact.
 (ii) *A* makes a bridge shape which his partner negotiates by going under and through the spaces thus formed.
(iii) *A* makes a shape which *B* has to assess and negotiate appropriately. *A* changes his shape and *B* adjusts accordingly.

94

(iv) Continuous interchanging is a development from (iii).
A makes himself the obstacle to be negotiated by *B*, and so on.
As the pupils become adept, this interchanging should be one
of split-second timing and continuity.

LESSON A

Theme

Working with a partner without contact

Limbering

In twos. *A* travels making straight line patterns on the floor. *B*
follows on exactly the same track.

Teaching: (i) The pathway made by *A* should be clearly defined
and not complicated.

(ii) The action chosen by *A* need not be copied by *B*.

Movement training

Task 1

In twos, copying a short sequence. *A* and *B* each perform a
simple sequence; one is chosen and the partner attempts to
copy it exactly.

Teaching: (i) The two children choose the relationship they
prefer, i.e. following, mirroring or in canon.

(ii) The sequence must be clear in action and unchanged when
repeated.

Task 2

In twos, *A* makes a shape (curled; with legs wide apart; close
to the floor, etc.). *B* negotiates.

Teaching: (i) The shape selected by *A* must be clear and simple.

(ii) Encourage variety and ingenuity in both the shape-making
and the negotiating.

Apparatus work

Group 1   Two benches and two mats

Task

The children start at a given point, X, and work parallel to each other.

Teaching: (i) Accuracy of timing is important here. Encourage pupils to practise on the floor while waiting their turn on the apparatus.

(ii) The pupils work independently. The only restriction is that they should keep parallel with each other.

Group 2   Box and mats

Task

Copy a partner's action on and off the box.

Teaching: (i) Keen observation is required by *B* if his partner's actions are to be copied accurately.

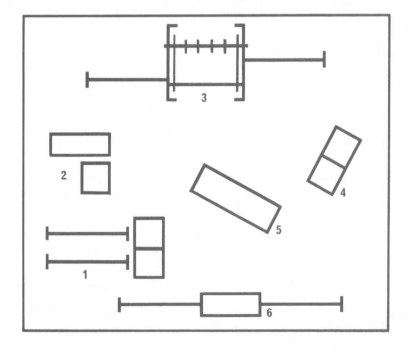

(ii) Each child should have the opportunity of being leader.

*Group 3   Climbing frame, ladder and pole fixed across bay,
                two inclined benches*
Task

Follow a partner's pathway.

Teaching: Here it is only the pathway that is dictated by the leader. Encourage a variety of actions appropriate to the apparatus.

Group 4   Two mats
Task

In twos, explore the possibilities of working 'in time' and transferring weight.

Teaching: As the emphasis is on timing and rhythm, movements involved in the transference of weight should be uncomplicated.

Group 5   Mattress
Task

In twos, *A* adopts a shape to be negotiated by *B* in a contrasting way. *B* then becomes the obstacle to be negotiated by *A*.

Teaching: If *A* adopts a curled position, *B* negotiates by an action involving stretching. (Alternatively this task could be negotiation by matching the shape of the obstacle.)

Group 6   Box or table and two benches
Task

In twos, start at a given point, X, meet on the box and pass each other to finish in your partner's starting position.

Teaching: (i) This task involves sharing the top of the box, so suitable actions must be chosen so that the pair can pass safely.

(ii) Accurate timing is necessary for the passing to take place on the box. Encourage continuous and flowing movement.

Working in contact with a partner

1. One pupil acts as a stable base for the other to push off from or fly over. Leap-frog is an example of this type of work in twos. The child who is the 'apparatus' must be in a steady position and unyielding when the full weight of the partner is felt.

2. Balancing on a partner is another way in which one bears the weight of the other, e.g. *A* kneels on all fours, *B* puts his arms under *A*'s waist and by pushing off strongly from his feet achieves an inverted balanced position. It is important that *A* should remain firm and unyielding as *B* moves into the balance.

3. Helping a partner to jump. This is seen when one pupil helps the other to get higher and to stay in the air longer than would otherwise be possible. The supporter must take up a position with a wide, steady base and be able to remain firm yet add to the thrust upward as his partner jumps. It is important that the supporter should know where contact will be made, so that the base can be adjusted accordingly to be of maximum stability.

Pushing and pulling in twos

Children enjoy pushing and pulling contests such as when, with the palms of the hands in contact, one partner attempts to push the other backwards; or when in a tug-of-war the aim is to pull the opponent over a line marked on the floor. Other ways of holding each other and pushing against each other give added interest. The pupils will discover the necessity for a wide stance, with the feet gripping the floor firmly. They will also need to use their legs with resilience, to adjust to the changing pressures of the pushing and pulling.

LESSON B

Theme

Working with a partner

Limbering

In twos; practise freely negotiating your partner as an obstacle.

Teaching: Encourage continuity in changing from being the obstacle to being the performer.

Movement training
Task 1

In twos. Take a partner's weight. *A* selects a stable position on which *B* balances.

Teaching: The shape which *A* adopts must afford a stable base for balancing and yet be comfortable to maintain. *A* must be firm and unyielding from start to finish of *B*'s moving to achieve and come out of balance.

Task 2

In twos. Use your partner to achieve flight.

Teaching: (i) *A* must adopt a firm, unyielding position as the 'apparatus' to be pushed away from.

(ii) The push-off by *B* must be firm but of short duration. (Leap-frog is likely here, but one can push off from other parts of the body, e.g. thighs and hips. If the former, the push can be from the foot of the performer who uses the thigh as a raised jumping-off base.)

Apparatus work

Group 1   Mats
Task

In twos. Start opposite each other at the edge of the mat. Work on a sequence which involves crossing and recrossing the mat.

Teaching: This task offers the pair ample opportunity for inventiveness as they can pass each other, negotiate each other as an obstacle, perform mirror actions, etc.

Group 2   Inclined bench, bar box and mat
Task

In twos. Follow the leader, matching pathway and actions.

Teaching: (i) Actions must be uncomplicated and clearly performed.

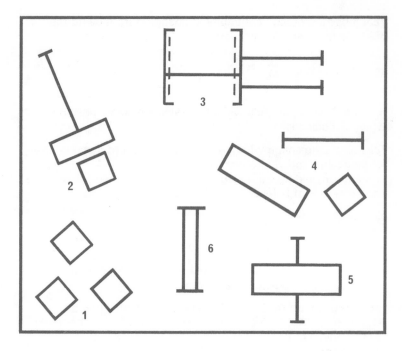

(ii) Encourage the pupils to approach the apparatus from various directions.

Group 3   *Climbing frame, ladder or bench fixed across bay, and two inclined benches*
Task

Use all the apparatus but work parallel on the benches and match your actions on the ladder/bench.

Teaching : (i) The benches may be used to mount or come off from the apparatus.

(ii) Ensure a firm grip on both the frame and the ladder.

(iii) Matching actions on the ladder will necessitate one child following the other.

Group 4   *Bench, table and mat with gaps between*
Task

In twos. Partners assist each other to cross the gaps.

Teaching : The gaps should be sufficiently wide to offer a challenge. The pupils will be required to discuss ways of tackling the problem. Sometimes one partner will assist by acting as a 'stepping-stone'; at other times it will be a case of assisting a jump.

Group 5   *Mattress laid over bench*
Task

In twos. Practise 'diving' over the bench and rolling on the mat in time with each other.

Teaching : (i) This task can be done either side by side, facing in the same direction, or starting from opposite sides of the bench. Whichever method is selected, timing must be judged accurately.

(ii) Whenever the hands touch the mattress, the weight is transferred to the shoulders and back.

Group 6   *Four benches arranged as a platform* (*two on two*)
Task

In twos. Work together sharing the apparatus.

Teaching : Pupils can work together, alongside each other, or from opposite ends of the apparatus. The hands should be placed flat, not gripping the underside of a top bench, as the bench may in these circumstances move.

PART III

Organisation

Prior to the lesson

'If pupils are confident and feel secure, they learn more readily.' This statement is frequently heard or read and is very true, but it speaks only of the pupils. What of the teacher? One hears students and teachers say, 'I don't like taking P.Ed. because I don't know what the children are going to do', or 'I never allow the pupils to use apparatus because I am afraid'. Because the teacher is lacking in confidence the pupils are denied an essential part of their educational programme. How then can these persons become confident in their teaching? Probably this lack of confidence is due mainly to a lack of organisation. This shortcoming is not deliberate; it arises from a false argument which runs like this: 'All children love to move, physical education involves moving *so* the pupils will have a good lesson if they are allowed to move.' The truth is that without organisation there can be nothing more than a kind of playtime.

It is precisely because children love to move that organisation is essential. They must learn to move and so move to learn.

What requires to be organised? Firstly, the thoughts of the teacher prior to the lesson. She will decide why she is going to teach what she is going to teach. But is this sufficient?

In all subject areas within the Primary school programme, lessons have to be prepared beforehand. The subject matter has to be thought out; the materials to be used by the teacher and the pupils must be considered; and the responses of the pupils must be anticipated, i.e. 'If I ask this question, what answers am I likely to get from the class? Will these answers give me the lead I require to proceed to the next stage?'

A similar technique is necessary prior to the teaching of inventive movement, e.g. 'If I set the task, "Move freely over the floor on hands and feet", what responses can I expect?'

If the teacher thinks about this beforehand she will be prepared for a variety of responses, viz. moving two hands followed by two feet; moving alternate hands and feet; moving in different directions; moving quickly or slowly; moving with the front of the body uppermost; twisting when travelling freely, etc., etc.

Because the teacher has thought about the likely responses, she will be prepared with helpful and constructive teaching points. She will not then say, 'I don't know what the children are going to do'.

Similarly with tasks involving apparatus, e.g.

Apparatus   Climbing frame with bench fixed across bay and one inclined bench

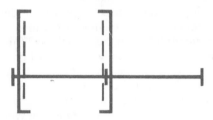

Task

Use the apparatus and show at least two ways of transferring your weight. What might the teacher expect the pupils to do here?

A pupil might:
 (i) Climb up the outside of the frame, slide through the space opposite the bench, walk along the bench and clamber through to walk down the inclined bench.

(ii) Climb up inside the frame to step on to the bench, sit with legs astride and 'bump' himself along, clamber on to the inclined bench and slide down with legs astride.

(iii) Pull himself up the inclined bench and through to the horizontal one, pull himself along and then climb down the frame.

(iv) Twist in and out of the spaces on the frame, twist to grip the bench from underneath and travel along in monkey-like fashion, pull himself up to move through the frame feet first and slide down the bench.

(v) Scramble up the underside of the inclined bench, through the frame and twist on to the top of the bench, roll along, move through the opposite space on the frame and slowly lower the body to the floor hands first.

(vi) Climb the upright of the frame and step on to the bench, travel along it on hands and feet and slide down the inclined bench in a prone position.
etc., etc.

By anticipating responses of this kind, the teacher will be ready to give the necessary coaching and guidance. Consider each of the above in turn:

(i) This is a rather pedestrian response. The teacher should be ready to encourage the child to be more adventurous, with the question, 'Can you change level as you travel on the bench?' Thus the child would try something other than a simple walking action.

(ii) Sitting with legs astride is used on both benches. After the child has done this successfully more than once, he should be asked to find other ways of transferring his weight on the horizontal bench.

(iii) This child obviously likes to keep close to the supporting surface but should be encouraged to find other ways of travelling. 'Can you cross the bench on your hands and feet?' This way of moving keeps the child in contact with the bench but his weight is no longer fully supported along it, so there is now a true transference of weight and a different experience for the child.

(iv) In sliding down a bench children tend to slide on their seat with their knees bent and their feet raised off the bench. As speed increases, however, they suddenly put their feet flat on the bench. The upper part of the body continues to move and is therefore jerked forward. The teacher should train the children to keep their feet off the bench throughout the slide.

(v) This is a good solution involving a variety of movements. Children choosing this solution are obviously confident on apparatus and need only be reminded about gripping firmly.

(vi) This child shows initiative in making use of the upright edge of the frame and in being prepared to climb above the level of the bench in order to step on to it. While the child is sliding in the prone position, his head should be held high. Obviously the far end of the bench must be clear of any obstruction.

It is advisable, when planning apparatus arrangements, to do more than make a few sketches on a piece of paper. Time spent in the hall at lunch-time or after school and with the help of a colleague, the janitor or willing pupils in setting up a new arrangement will enable the teacher to see the arrangement three-dimensionally, i.e. as it will be when the pupils embark upon the set task. She can now look critically at the arrangement in the light of the task or, conversely, reassess the problem contained in the wording of the task. It not infrequently happens that a task as set down on paper appears reasonable, yet when the children tackle it built-in difficulties become apparent.

Example

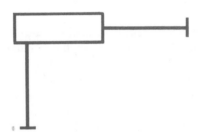

Apparatus   Bar box and two inclined benches

Task

Travel along a bench, mount the box with hands leading, travel over the box by rolling curled up.

This apparatus arrangement looks reasonable on paper and the task seems quite appropriate. The teacher will discover, however, that though the length of the box is more than adequate for rolling, the same cannot be said of the width. It is too narrow and so a child anxious to answer the task as stated will attempt to roll and may fall off the box. Had the teacher set up this arrangement prior to the lesson she would have seen the relative distances, reworded her task and added a mat to the arrangement.

Task

A and B show starting points. Choose one and travel along the bench by transferring weight; mount the box and use it to jump high; land and roll over the mat.

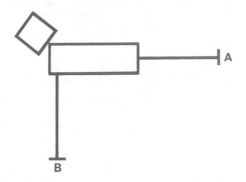

A situation of this kind arising in the course of such an active lesson is bound to undermine the teacher's confidence. This will not occur if the actual apparatus arrangement and the task have been looked at together. It is also most helpful if the teacher herself attempts to answer the task on the apparatus arrangement. She will then be more aware of what she is asking her pupils to do.

At the same time she can very quickly see whether the place chosen for an arrangement is appropriate or whether, for example, the inclined bench is too close to the wall and consequently unsafe for a child sliding down it.

As is generally known, children do not all the time respond according to expectation, but if one is prepared for most contingencies the unexpected will not upset the overall plan— nor the teacher's confidence. Children in a secure atmosphere do not attempt what they think they may not be able to achieve; but neither do they opt out. They find a way of answering the task. Next time they will move one step—or perhaps two— towards an alternative solution which is more difficult and at the same time more satisfying. One can see this process in action. It is easy to discern which solution a child has selected. He may decide to modify it, at the crucial moment taking an easier route, but, given the opportunity he will return to the problem and by improving his skill and so gaining confidence he will eventually achieve what he wanted to do in the first instance. He has explored various possibilities, discovered what he can do, selected what is the best solution for himself and by practice and repetition improved his skill and consolidated his achievement. These four steps—exploration, discovery, selection and consolidation—form the learning process in inventive movement.

The teacher's planning must allow for this. Too often the pupils are told to move to the next apparatus arrangement before they have had time to find out what they can achieve at the one they are working on. This hurrying along is the result of the teacher's desire to see each child work at every apparatus arrangement in one lesson. However, her aim defeats the purpose of apparatus work and her undue haste causes the pupils to feel rushed and become careless in the way in which they move in relation to the apparatus. Pupils should be encouraged to improve their skill by being given sufficient time to explore the possibilities within the task and to come to their own solution. This is essential to their learning and to their sense of security.

Apparatus work

Handling apparatus

Children should be trained to handle and assemble gymnastic apparatus. The time spent in this training ensures that in future the equipment will be handled with safety and efficiency.

The teacher should check all apparatus arrangements and in particular make sure that the climbing frame is stable, with all the bolts securely home, before allowing anyone to use it. In some schools it is one of the janitor's daily duties to set up the climbing frame for the day. Each teacher should, however, check the bolts as not infrequently pupils passing through the hall are tempted to unfasten one or two!

All apparatus must be carried, never dragged, across the floor. Pupils carrying items of equipment should walk facing forward and the number handling each piece should be between two and four, never more as then they hinder each other's progress.

The following methods of carrying equipment will be found to be most efficient.

110

Benches : Two pupils facing the direction of travel ; bench held at hip height with one hand gripping each side of the bench.

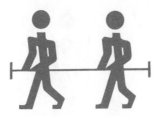

Mats : Two pupils facing the direction of travel, one at each end of the folded mat.

Four pupils, one at each corner, if mats are particularly cumbersome.

Bar box : Top layer—four pupils, two on each side facing forward ; nearside hand grips under box top, offside hand rests on top to maintain balance :

Second layer—two pupils, one on each side facing forward ; nearside hand grips middle bar.

Canes: Canes must always be carried upright and held by the person's side:

The essential procedure is that at all times those pupils who are carrying apparatus should face in the direction of travel. If this is not done there is the danger that a child who is walking backwards may trip and a piece of heavy equipment may fall on top of him.

Positioning apparatus

If possible large pieces of apparatus should be used fairly near to where they are stored. This avoids a long carry, perhaps to the opposite end of the hall. Time spent carrying and assembling equipment is time lost in using it. This time must be allowed for when planning the lesson, but careful organisation will ensure that it is kept to a minimum.

Apparatus should be positioned in such a way that all the available space is efficiently used. Each apparatus arrangement should have an area of floor space around it which children can use while waiting their turn. Careful siting of apparatus will enable the teacher to move freely from group to group coaching and giving encouragement. Also it is essential that even when giving her immediate attention to one group she should at the same time be able to see the other children at work and thus make any comment which may be required at that particular moment.

Careful planning will ensure that there will be no danger of children landing near obstructions such as doors, walls, windows, or other pieces of equipment.

Grouping pupils for apparatus work

Groups can be formed in several ways, each method having its own merit. The important point, whichever method is adopted, is that the groups should remain essentially the same and not be formed afresh every week. Belonging to a group is important for the child and for the group, the members of which share the apparatus, co-operate with each other and so feel secure in this familiar and close-knit environment. There will be occasions when it may be necessary to change one or two children from one group to another but this should not disrupt the working harmony. Another, rather mundane, reason for grouping the same children together is the saving of time which would be needed if the children were to be regrouped each lesson. Each child knows where his own group place is and this in itself allows the teacher to check the number in each group. Having group places for pupils helps to strengthen discipline and control. It may be necessary on occasion to require the pupils to stop working and return to their group places if there has been a severe breach of discipline.

It is recommended that in the early stages the pupils return to their own group place at the end of apparatus work and put away the apparatus they set up. This allows the pupils to become proficient in the handling and assembling of one arrangement before learning to cope with others.

Suggestions for grouping:

(i) Children form themselves into groups of the required number.

(ii) Pupils work in the same groups as those already in operation in the classroom.

(iii) Groups are composed of children of approximately the same age if vertical or family grouping is a feature of the school.

(iv) Upper Primary groups can be composed of boys' groups and girls' groups if this segregation is thought to be necessary. There are marked differences in the way in which boys and girls of this age and at this stage of development tackle problems involving physical skill. The boys seem to prefer to approach a task by methods involving strength and speed, whereas the girls are more concerned with poise and precision. If teachers feel that these preferences are not conducive to group harmony an adjustment to boys' groups and girls' groups should be made.

113

The number of groups in a class will depend on the amount of apparatus available and the number of pupils. Throughout this book reference has been made to six groups, but this number should not be thought of as invariable.

Group work must be included in every lesson but should never be the sole activity in a lesson. Movement training or floor work must always precede work with large apparatus.

Programming apparatus work

There are many ways in which apparatus work can be introduced, but where pupils are unfamiliar with large apparatus the following programme will be found helpful.

Stage 1

The class works in six groups using one type of apparatus. It is suggested that mats should be used, partly because they are easy to carry but more fundamentally because the responses to the tasks will most probably involve various types of rolling, jumping and rolling, and other methods of transferring the weight all of which are essential to the safe management of the body in motion.

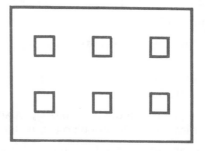

Task suggestions

(i) Find different ways of rolling over the mat.

(ii) Jump on to the mat and roll over.

(iii) Approach your mat from any direction and find ways of crossing it with your feet high.

Stage 2

The class works in the same groups but now uses two types of apparatus.

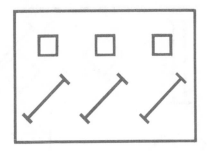

Tasks

Mats

(i) Start from one corner and travel backwards to the opposite corner.

(ii) How far across the mat can you jump?

(iii) Find ways of moving across the mat stretching as far away from it as possible.

Benches

(i) Travel along the bench using your hands and feet.

(ii) Can you make a zigzag pattern as you travel from end to end?

(iii) Find out if you can move under as well as over the bench.

The groups interchange by moving across the hall.

Stage 3

A greater variety of apparatus can now be introduced and it can be placed in such a way as to allow for full use of the space available.

The class works in six groups:

1 and 4 using a bench and mat,

2 and 5 using different apparatus (benches, box top) but working on the same task,

3 and 6 using a mat.

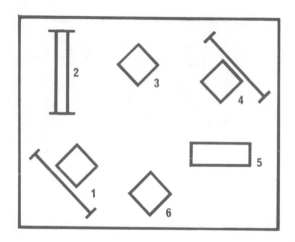

Task suggestions

Groups 1 and 4   Move from the bench to the mat with hands leading. Roll on the mat.

Groups 2 and 5   Find different ways of mounting, travelling along and getting off the apparatus.

Groups 3 and 6   Practise 'collapsing' on the mat.

Groups 1, 2 and 3   Interchange on a circular pathway while 4, 5 and 6 do likewise.

Stage 4

The apparatus arrangement will be the same as in Stage 3 except that the climbing frame will take the place of one of the mats (whichever is nearer the frame). As each group starts working on the climbing frame the teacher should give most of her immediate attention to that particular group, the other pupils being allowed to work independently on apparatus with which they are familiar.

In the first instance there should be no formal task for the group at the climbing frame. They must be free to explore this piece of apparatus and become familiar with it. (Infants frequently sit on one of the bars and do little else but look around. This is quite acceptable, as later on they will begin to move in order to further their exploration.)

Groups should now rotate thus:

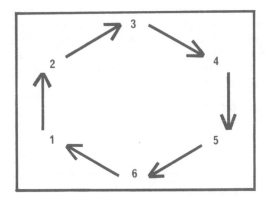

Each group should be given the opportunity to work with at least two apparatus arrangements in each lesson. In the lesson following the teacher must ensure that after the apparatus has been set up the pupils should move round and begin on a new arrangement.

Apparatus assignment cards

When working with young children who cannot read or understand written instructions the teacher should tell each group which pieces of apparatus are required, where they are to be placed and what she wishes the pupils to do. It should not be necessary to reiterate every detail each time the same apparatus arrangements are set out, if in the classroom there is displayed the large-scale plan of the arrangements in current use. The description of this plan is given in Part 1 (page 15). Reference to this plan before the lesson will remind the pupils of where their apparatus is placed. As apparatus work follows on from the previous lesson the teacher will be able to say 'Go to your group places, get out the apparatus and begin working'.

When the children have reached the stage of reading competently, apparatus assignment cards should be used. The pupils will need to be introduced to these cards in the same manner as to work cards used in the classroom situation. This introduction should be made in the classroom so that time is not lost during the lesson in the hall. While the children are going to their group places one child from each group should collect the apparatus assignment card and return to the group which then decides who will carry and place the apparatus. It is essential that all wording on the card, especially the instructions for the task, should be clear and concise, otherwise too much time is spent interpreting the instructions. Each card should show:

(*a*) The group number
(*b*) The apparatus to be collected
(*c*) The apparatus arrangement
(*d*) The task.

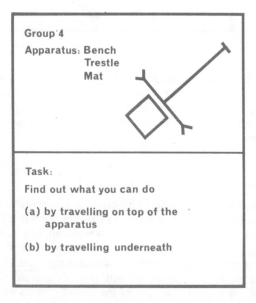

Group 4

Apparatus: Bench
              Trestle
              Mat

Task:

Find out what you can do

(a) by travelling on top of the apparatus

(b) by travelling underneath

These apparatus assignment cards can be plain postcards or cut from coloured card which is available in all schools. When the groups are ready to change over, the card should be left for the next group on or close by the equipment.

Improvised apparatus

When improvised apparatus is used to supplement the supply of gymnastic equipment, each teacher must ensure that it is stable, strong enough to bear a pupil's weight, and splinter-free.

Trestle-tables or ordinary school tables can be used for many tasks, especially those involving rolling and jumping. The spaces underneath the apparatus also offer scope for inventiveness.

Chairs are useful as items of improvised apparatus, but as they are inclined to tip if placed in the conventional way, care should be taken in the selection of the task.

Stools and strong wooden boxes are also very suitable. Ammunition boxes (ex-government supplies) are excellent, being strong and usually with rope handles.

Planks and ladders allow for a variety of uses: they can be supported on or across tables, trestles, boxes, or stools and chairs.

Safety precautions

Teachers are naturally concerned with the safety of the pupils in their care. When all essential precautions are taken inventive movement is no more dangerous for the pupils than moving around the classroom where many more obstacles have to be negotiated within a much more confined space, viz. desks, chairs, school bags lying on the floor and sundry other items which make constant manœuvring necessary.

What are these essential precautions?

(i) Discipline and control at all times. If the lesson is well-planned and the work is sufficiently interesting and challenging the children will work confidently and with concentration.

(ii) If the floor surface is splinter-free children may work with bare feet, otherwise well-fitting gym shoes are essential. No child should be permitted to take part while wearing socks, stockings or tights without gym shoes. Gym shoes with laces lost or untied are also a potential source of danger. Outdoor shoes of course should never be allowed. They are highly dangerous to the wearer and, in addition, they ruin the floor surface.

(iii) Apparatus must be safe. It must be stable, securely fixed and

119

splinter-free. Any piece of equipment found to be in need of repair must be withdrawn from use immediately.

(iv) Pupils must be trained to handle and carry apparatus carefully. Gymnastic apparatus should be used only during a lesson and not at break-time or lunch-time unless under the supervision of a teacher.

A final word to the Primary school teacher for whom this book is written: approach your teaching of inventive movement with well-planned lessons, with interest and enthusiasm and be sure in the knowledge that as your pupils learn to move so they will move and learn and enjoy doing so.